Raising the Standards

Through Chapter Books: The C.I.A. Approach

Sarah Collinge

PEANUT BUTTER
PUBLISHING

Seattle, Washington
Portland, Oregon
Denver, Colorado
Vancouver, B.C.
Scottsdale, Arizona
Minneapolis, Minnesota

Peanut Butter Publishing
943 NE Boat Street
Seattle, Washington 98105
206-860-4900
www.peanutbutterpublishing.com

To my mother, who instilled in me

a passion for literacy,

a love of learning,

and the joy of teaching.

Thank you for inspiring me to achieve my dreams.

Table of Contents

Acknowledgements

As a young child, I dreamed of someday becoming either a teacher or a writer. Teaching and writing were interests instilled in me by my mother, who gave up teaching to raise twin daughters and who to this day harbors a dream to write. I always thought I would become one or the other, a teacher *or* a writer. Imagine my surprise when God placed it on my heart to be both.

So here I am, a passionate teacher and newly established author—proof that when you believe in yourself and have the lavish support of truly amazing people, you will be blessed.

This book began as an opportunity to reflect on the incredible experience I was given coaching teachers in literacy in the Mukilteo School District, in Washington State. Without those two years of intense professional training and hours of work in classrooms K–6, I would not have the synthesis of knowledge that I bring to this book. Therefore, I would like to thank the incredibly talented professionals who were a part of that team.

First, I am forever grateful to Mary Beth Crowder-Meyer, whose voice guided me as I wrote this book and whose mentorship was foundational to my pedagogy. It was such an honor to receive the rich training in the field of literacy that she gave me.

I have so much gratitude for Dr. Lloy Schaaf, whose professionalism I have always admired and aspired to. Lloy believed in my potential, supported me in my growth, and gave me the opportunity to enrich my career. It has truly been an honor for me to work with her.

I have been fortunate enough to have the support of two outstanding building principals. I have great respect for the creative, visionary thinking of Leslie Clauson, whose vision for Horizon Elementary School was what propelled me into this work. Leslie instilled in me a desire to make my teaching explicit and rigorous, and her mentorship has been invaluable. Rosalynn Schott's leadership and mentorship has also been a wonderful gift. I'm grateful to her for supporting me during the infant stages of my research, having faith in my instructional decisions, and allowing me the opportunity to have leadership in her building.

I'm immensely grateful for my coaching team—Alisa Griffen, Steve Raymond, Laura Reidt, Elizabeth McAllister, and Lori Sinning—and for the insightful conversations that we had in the hours that we spent sitting at the round table, reflecting on coaching cycles and planning our work together. Those conversations became the idea bank for this book. This book represents our two years of work together.

I'd like to also thank Linda Kendall and Jennifer Burd, for their faithful support in launching workshops and professional development opportunities.

In addition, I would like to thank all of the teachers who were gracious enough to allow me into their classrooms. Our reflective conversations enriched me beyond measure. I feel extreme gratitude for the opportunity to have worked with such talented professionals. I especially thank those teachers who volunteered so much of their time in coaching cycles and after-school workshops. I remain humbled by their eagerness to join me in my work.

Key teachers were involved in the research for this book. They welcomed me into their classrooms when the C. I. A. approach was just a theory. They let me (often with my video camera in hand) take over their classrooms. Thank you to Teri DeCocq, Sandy Bajczuk, Dawn Halvorson, Heather Neal, and Christina Fulkerson. Thank you to Paula Miklosovic and Diane Plesha, whom I had the pleasure of teaching with at Discovery Elementary School and who were early pilot testers of the first unit of study for fifth grade. They both provided guidance, support, and friendship, above and beyond. I can't thank them enough for taking a risk, spending their hard-earned pennies on used books, and sharing my thinking about teaching and learning. They are cherished friends, and I will certainly miss our days teaching together.

I also want to thank the fifth- and sixth-grade teachers at Mattawa Elementary, especially Paul Voorhees and Darlene James.

Thank you also to Thom Garrard, for lending and giving so many books to this work and for sharing his love of books with me. Thank you to Shelley Santti, for being a friend and coach who is always there when I need enriching conversation and thoughtful reflection.

A special thank you to the members of my original third-grade team—Nikole Jansen, Angie Georgeadis, Anja Rossiter, and Deanna Fischer—who supported me through difficult times and encouraged me through the best times. I gleaned so much knowledge from them, and I have the fondest memories of our time teaching together and of the girls' nights that got me through writing this book!

Most important, I would like to thank all my students. Their individual stories, which I've found so inspiring, are woven into the pages of this book. I am proud of and believe in each and every one of them. I want to thank them for teaching me; I have learned more from them than they will ever know, and I hope that this book inspires them to achieve their greatest dreams.

I would like to acknowledge Dr. Nancy Johnson, who developed my interest in children's literature and who gave me the early foundation of my professional pedagogy by demonstrating the value of read-aloud as a central component of classroom literacy. Much of the literature that she read aloud, I later had the joy of sharing with my students.

This book is written in memory of Susan Atwell, my Bible study leader and dear friend. Susan introduced me to the inductive method authored by Kay Arthur (1994). Immediately, I saw the parallelism between the way Arthur teaches us to read our Bible and the methods I outline in this book. Susan's dedicated mentoring and friendship launched many of the C. I. A. strategies. I am ever grateful to her, and miss her dearly.

I am so very thankful for Elliott Wolf, my publishing consultant. He has been invaluable in guiding me through the unknown regions of this work. He's always there to answer my call, and I have grown to look forward to our daily check-ins over the phone. By the time this is over, I am sure we will be related—if not by blood, then by sweat and tears (of joy).

Thank you to the amazing team of professionals who brought this book to life, especially Martha Goelzer, my editor, and David Marty and Amy Vaughn of Soundview Design.

Finally, I would like to thank members of my family for their immense and generous support. Special thanks to Larry, Maggie, and Iris Collinge, for their love and encouragement, and to my parents, who gave me the courage to achieve my dream. My mother, Nancy Wolf, instilled in me a love of reading that began in my early childhood. My father, John Wolf, gifted me business knowledge and an entrepreneurial spirit. Both of my parents have dedicated their time and talents to helping me bring this book to publication. I am so grateful for their willingness to work hard. I love them both!

A loving thank you to my husband, Max, for his unfailing love and generous support. I believe this journey has brought us even closer together. Throughout the countless hours that I have committed to writing this book, Max has taken care of the household and has been a wonderful father to our two children, Hannah and Sadie.

Finally, this book would not have been written without the professional knowledge and emotional support provided by Bethany Robinson, who is both my colleague and identical twin sister. I have so much respect for her knowledge of literacy and her natural, instinctive talent for working with teachers. I have learned so much from her— her wise thinking permeates the pages of this book. Throughout this process, she has been not only my best friend and sister, but also my instructional coach, professional assistant, editor, sales representative, and (not my favorite) taskmaster. She is also co-author of the C. I. A. Units of Study that accompany this book. It is with joy and honor that I stand side by side with her in this work.

Introduction

It is the beginning of the school year, and as I unpack boxes of September supplies, I find a poster sent to me by a local bookstore, intended for tracking students' completion of books. With good intentions, I hang this poster up in my classroom and write all my students' names on the chart. As the first week commences, I plan to spend much of my time laying the foundation of independent reading by teaching students how to select "just right" books and how to set goals for what they will read this year. This work starts in conversations, in both whole-group discussions and one-on-one at my conference table.

Identifying Trends

Before my small groups begin, I spend much of the independent reading time conferring with readers. The purpose of these conferences is to find out who my students are as readers—what books they like to read, what strategies they know and use, and how they think and talk about books. Every year I am shocked at the lack of intention and purpose my fifth-graders have as they begin reading self-selected books. All of them are reading chapter books and carefully selecting texts at their independent reading levels. Yet, after reading the first few chapters, many of my students are unable to tell me the most critical information about their books. They are reading with the misconception that, at some point, the books will magically make sense to them. Unfortunately, no one can read by magic, and therefore I know that these students will begin the cyclical process of selecting and abandoning text.

I want my students to read with engagement and purpose, rather than by magic. But what does that type of reading look like in the context of a chapter book, and how do I teach it? To understand the process, I return to my conference table.

Damon's Story

It is day two of my reading workshop, and for the first time, my students are going into the classroom library to shop for books. I have spent two days discussing how readers pick a "just right" book based on level and interest. I know that for many, these lessons will need to be retaught repeatedly throughout the year. I pick up my notebook and begin to observe students as they select books, jotting down notes as I watch.

Damon walks over to the library and immediately approaches the book bin containing the Last Dragon Chronicles. He quickly grabs the first book, *Firestar* (D'Lacey, 2007), and heads back to his seat. He opens the book and begins reading page one. At this point, I am curious. Did he know what he wanted to read before he went back to my library? What made him pick that Chronicle? Is this book going to be too difficult for him? I quickly make a note to conference with him within the week.

The next day, I pull Damon back to my conference table and begin our discussion about his book choice. He tells me that he picked this book because his cousin recommended it to him. He is clearly very excited to read the book. I ask him to open up to the page he is at, and he begins to read aloud. I take careful notes to determine whether the book is at his "just right" level. Because he makes only three errors on the page, I know he is in the right book. But I am still concerned about its length. In two days of independent reading, Damon has read only four pages. With this kind of pace, I know it will be difficult for him to sustain his interest over the length of the text.

The question becomes this: How do I help students develop the stamina to read longer texts? I know this isn't just about Damon's book choice. It is about the many students in my classroom who, despite their interest, are unable to finish longer texts. It is about helping them take the large goal of finishing a book such as *Firestar* (D'Lacey, 2007) and dividing that goal into manageable pieces.

Alex's Story

Next, I approach Alex, who has decided to read the first book in the Warriors series, *Into the Wild* (Hunter, 2003). He already has a good start on the book after taking it home for nightly reading. He is well into chapter 3, and he communicates to me that it is feeling "just right" for him. I begin by asking him some basic questions about the story, including questions about the main character. Alex easily shares, but he excludes the character's name. I stop him in his description and inquire about the name. He is stumped. Alex, like many other students whom I conference with, has failed to recognize the importance of recalling important information about the main character. Without my intervention, Alex would continue reading the book while missing a largely important piece of understanding.

I quickly note that if I am going to help readers access longer, more complex texts, I must begin by helping them collect critical information early in those texts: character, setting, and plot.

Brisa's Story

Later in the week, I sit next to Brisa, an on-grade-level reader, who is reading one of the Judy Moody books by Megan McDonald. I quickly note that she has already switched books, abandoning her first book choice, *Olive's Ocean* by Kevin Henkes (2005). I settle into our conference by asking her what prompted her to switch books. Brisa indicates that *Olive's Ocean* was too hard and that she likes reading books in the Judy Moody series because she read many of them in fourth grade. This is a common trend that emerges in intermediate classrooms: students abandoning grade-level texts to return to comfortable series books. I take note of Brisa's words and continue our discussion. I'm interested in what makes Judy Moody a comfortable series for Brisa. I quickly get my answer.

Brisa begins to tell me everything she knows about Judy Moody. She understands this character's circumstance and knows why this character behaves the way she does. She also recognizes the predictability of the plot across the many books in this series. Before reading this new Judy Moody book, Brisa already knows exactly how the book will go. Brisa, like all readers, finds comfort in predictability.

Rising to the Challenge

At this point, I feel like a detective who has been investigating a crime. Common trends across my classroom have emerged, and I know the pitfalls students face as they launch into grade-level-appropriate texts.

1. My students have not built the stamina for reading longer texts and need support in setting manageable goals.

2. My students do not have an understanding of the comprehension work readers do while reading longer texts and of how that work is similar to or different from what they have learned to do in shorter texts. The use of comprehension strategies in complex text will need to be explicitly taught in order to help bridge this learning gap.

3. My students do not know the predictable elements within each genre, and they therefore gravitate back to easy series books. Therefore, I will need to teach genres so that they become predictable and comfortable for my students in the same way that series are.

I know these trends are all too familiar to you. I know this because I have had teachers share similar stories with me over the last six years of my research. It can be very overwhelming to see these habits and behaviors resurface every year, despite your consistent efforts to explicitly teach independent reading strategies. I am here to encourage you.

The last six years of my eleven years teaching have been spent researching in classrooms to determine how best to meet the needs of readers who are struggling to proficiently read increasingly difficult texts. I have sought to name the authentic processes expert readers use and to make these processes explicit for students. In my years as a classroom teacher, literacy coach, and literacy consultant, my theories grew out of the most current and most significant research findings. Focusing on best practices outlined in reports such as the *Report of the National Reading Panel* (National Institute of Child Health and Human Development [NICHHD], 2000), the ACT report *Reading Between the Lines* (2006), and the RAND Reading Study Group's *Reading for Understanding* (2002), and on findings published by the Common Core State Standards Initiative (CCSSI) (2010), I began to develop classroom instructional practices that promoted practices supported by research. Prioritizing my work at all times were the real-life interactions with students in classrooms of diverse learners.

The amount of knowledge I gained in these years of research was immense. Constantly challenged by new ideas and practices, I found myself returning to a simple list of priorities that proved central to increased literacy skills in my students—reading, writing, and talking intensively across the school day (Schmoker, 2011).

The C. I. A. approach to reading intends to force these priorities into our classrooms through core practices outlined in this book. In addition, the approach raises the standards we have outlined for students by allowing students to practice these standards in increasingly complex texts. Raising standards is not about redefining skills or strategies across grade levels. Raising standards is about applying the same strategies and skills in progressively more demanding texts.

The C. I. A. approach models the authentic habits of expert readers who are reading new genres or authors and who are selecting longer, more difficult texts. It breaks the reading process down into manageable steps of collecting critical information, interpreting the text, and applying the text to one's own life. This model blends the most current research findings with "old ideas and simple prescriptions—the key to better results" (Schmoker, 2011, Location 188).

Teachers who have implemented the C. I. A. model in their classrooms admit that they will no longer teach reading in any other way. Amazed by the engagement of their students and the impact of the approach on school and state test scores, they feel confident in the instruction they provide. For many, the approach puts the fun back into teaching.

In this book, you will read about each stage of the C. I. A. model and about how to use research-based classroom routines to support it. You will learn to use the gradual release model (Pearson & Gallagher, 1983), which can be used across instructional routines, to plan daily and long-term instruction. Primarily, I will discuss how to model the C. I. A. approach within an instructional read-aloud block, the time of the school day during which all students are exposed to demanding text levels through modeling and guided practice. As you read, you will be convinced that the C. I. A. approach is applicable to all readers, including struggling readers who, despite their reading levels, still need to be doing the thinking work demanded of them by grade-level texts.

Along the way, you will learn how readers keep notebooks that they can use as essential tools for comprehension. Student work samples will demonstrate how the level of thinking increases across texts, from strategy work to analysis and evaluation.

The work outlined in the C. I. A. model is new and innovative. Yet, the approach is backed by current research and implements rigorous standards outlined in our nation's Common Core State Standards (CCSSI, 2010). I believe that in reading this book, you will come to the conclusion that the C. I. A. approach is easy to implement, powerful, and effective. As a result, you will make this approach to teaching reading a priority in your classroom as you seek to align your instruction to increasing literacy demands. You will be amazed as your students become empowered to read and enjoy books as a lifelong habit. You may even begin to use this approach in your own, personal reading life, proving the program to be truly authentic to the work of expert readers.

Implementing Classroom Routines Grounded in Research

R esearch indicates that the demands that college, careers, and citizenship place on readers have either held steady or increased over roughly the last fifty years" (CCSSI, 2010, p. A2). This trend places new demands on students at all grade levels, as teachers work across grade-level spans to better prepare students for college readiness. At the same time, the texts used with students K–12 have decreased in complexity over the last half century as we have placed an increasing amount of pressure on teachers to "meet students where they are at." Unfortunately, the consequence of overfocusing on this accommodation has been low performance levels on college placement tests such as the ACT (ACT, 2009).

Too many students are impacted by low reading achievement. While intervention is important, it alone will not solve the problem. Students need to be able to read complex texts proficiently for success in high school, college, and the workplace. Reading these complex texts requires higher skill levels and stamina. "To grow, our students must read… lots of 'complex texts'—texts that offer them new language, new knowledge, and new modes of thought" (Adams, 2009, p. 189). It is a lack of training in how to comprehend complex texts that continues to keep students from college readiness, according to ACT findings (2009).

As the studies cited here imply, teachers, in alignment with increasing demands, must better prepare students for reading the complex texts required for college readiness. But how do teachers accomplish this with *all* students, including those who are struggling readers?

Using the Gradual Release Model as a Foundation

The Gradual Release of Responsibility Model (Pearson & Gallagher, 1983) is imperative as an instructional framework, moving students from explicit modeling toward independence through guided practice. Backed by a myriad of research, including work presented in the *Report of the National Reading Panel* (NICHHD, 2000), its ability to impact success is well known throughout the educational world.

The gradual release model must be the foundational piece on which we build our entire curriculum. Its purpose is to:

- Help students develop an understanding of the cognitive processes activated during reading, through teacher modeling.
- Model how readers utilize strategies to clarify and deepen comprehension.
- Guide students toward the use of these processes and strategies.
- Give students opportunities to safely practice these processes and strategies with teacher and partner assistance.
- Help readers gradually internalize these processes and strategies for independent mastery.

The gradual release model moves from teacher modeling to guided practice, peer practice, and independent practice. This instructional framework has been proven to increase reading comprehension in readers with a range of abilities (NICHHD, 2000).

In response to these research results, we should allow the gradual release model to define everything we do in our classrooms. We should consider this framework when designing a single lesson, an entire instructional block, a unit of study, or our year-long scope and sequence. What follows is a diagram that outlines the C. I. A. approach within a gradual release of responsibility model (Pearson & Gallagher, 1983).

Gradual Release of Responsibility

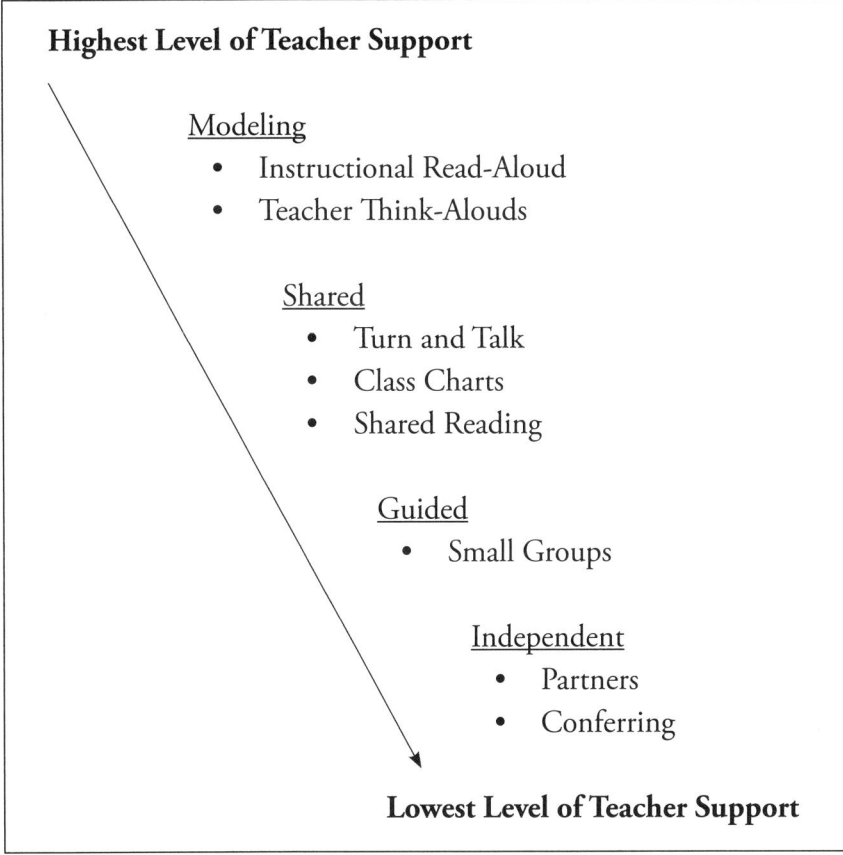

Highest Level of Teacher Support

<u>Modeling</u>
- Instructional Read-Aloud
- Teacher Think-Alouds

<u>Shared</u>
- Turn and Talk
- Class Charts
- Shared Reading

<u>Guided</u>
- Small Groups

<u>Independent</u>
- Partners
- Conferring

Lowest Level of Teacher Support

Adapted from the Gradual Release of Responsibility Model (Pearson & Gallagher, 1983)

As I anticipate the questions you might have as you read this book, I am certain that many of them could easily be answered through consideration of this model. Let the answers to your questions be guided by these key principals.

- Always begin your instruction with explicit teacher modeling.
- Provide guided practice through supported turn and talk.
- Provide additional guided practice through small group instruction and one-on-one conferring.
- Allow independent work to take its time—make sure students have received ample support in modeling and guided practice before expecting the work to be accomplished independently.
- When students struggle, take them back a step on the gradual release.

When teaching, we must always begin with and come back to explicit teacher modeling. Harvey and Goudvis use the metaphor of a beating heart to describe this motion, "where the balance between modeling instruction and guided practice pulses evenly back and forth" (2000, p. 31). Key structures that allow for this explicit teacher modeling include instructional read-aloud and shared reading. Because they provide unparalleled opportunities for explicit instruction, times spent in these activities should be cherished and valued in your classroom and building. Their significance can be communicated through both the classroom environment and the daily schedule.

The most coveted, protected time in a student's school day should be that in which he or she has the opportunity to listen and respond to quality literature that is at or above his or her grade level. Reading aloud, when conducted through an instructional focus, has been proven to improve listening comprehension, vocabulary, fluency, and motivation. "A well planned read aloud program, even for older students, can stimulate interest in books and introduce students to quality literature in various genres" (Rasinski, 2003, p. 40). Therefore, the instructional read-aloud is the vehicle through which we engage *all* students, despite their reading abilities, in the thinking demanded by complex text structures.

Communicating our Educational Values

As a literacy coach and literacy consultant, I have had the opportunity to work in a variety of classrooms across grade levels and schools. Walking into a classroom for the first time, I have often made assumptions about a teacher's values based on his or her classroom environment. Knowing this, on returning to my own classroom, I made sure that my values were being clearly communicated through purposeful classroom arrangements. I want students and guests to know, without a doubt, what my beliefs about teaching and learning are. Certainly, our classroom environment impacts and communicates our daily priorities.

The Meeting Area

Walk into my classroom and your eyes will immediately travel to our meeting area. This is the place in the room where we gather on the carpet for instructional read-aloud. Difficult to ignore, the meeting area takes up about a quarter of our classroom space and is decorated with an exuberant number of co-created charts. The space is defined by outlying furniture such as chairs and benches. A large rug creates a gathering place where students can sit crisscross. Anyone, student or guest, can see that my pedagogy centers on the gradual release of authentic reading habits from modeling, to guided practice, to independence.

A large carpet space devoted to read-aloud is not something one typically finds in a fifth-grade classroom, but for me, it is at the heart of what I do. This is the place where all my students, no matter their reading levels, meet to do the work of reading together. The intimacy of the meeting area communicates my belief in using shared experiences to support oral and written rehearsal. Foundational to the instructional read-aloud is the belief that reading is a social process and that "children learn best within a richly and rigorously interactive community" (Calkins, 2001, p. 13). Students are assigned partnerships and places to sit, ensuring that the learning gets started quickly. This well-defined space is where students gather on the floor or on benches to engage closely in the reading of good books.

While cozy, the meeting area is not a place to relax; it's a place for rigorous learning. This is communicated to the students through the positioning of the class easel, "the focal point of the meeting area" (Taberski, 2000, p. 21). Co-created charts are constructed daily on this easel and then moved to the large bulletin board space on the walls to either side. Displaying these charts in the meeting area is essential, as doing so turns them into tools that my students can access as they monitor and revise their comprehension while reading. In addition, these charts support the students as they transfer the work into small groups or independent reading.

Expectations for coming to the meeting area efficiently are modeled and practiced repeatedly throughout the year. Students come quickly with their reader's notebooks, read-aloud books, and pencils. Many of the students are anxious to get started—this is their favorite part of the instructional day.

Fifth-graders sit in the meeting area, ready for the read-aloud to begin.

Prioritizing our Schedules

Our priorities as educators are also detailed in the way we set up our daily schedules. Typically, subjects that hold the highest importance are given the largest, most coveted blocks of time within the instructional day. Therefore, when planning our schedules, we need to be cognizant of how our daily routines communicate our pedagogies.

Here is a sample fifth-grade block schedule that prioritizes reading:
8:55 Bell rings
9:00 **Read-Aloud Block**
9:45 **Reading Workshop**—Differentiated Instruction Block
  • Independent Reading
  • Conferring
  • Small-Group Instruction
  • Special Services (students might be pulled for reading intervention)
10:40 Plan Time Coverage
11:25 Math Block
12:20 Lunch
12:55 Math Workshop
2:00 Recess
2:15 **Content Area Literacy** (Social Studies, Science, Writing)
3:30 Dismiss

Protecting the Read-Aloud Block

Exposure to high levels of authentic literacy is critical to students' achievement (Schmoker, 2011). The instructional read-aloud should take place at a time when *all* students are in the room, including those who qualify for intervention. In many buildings across the country, this unfortunately is not a priority; some students are being pulled for special services and are rarely receiving instruction with grade-level texts at grade-level standards. While these students might make small gains in reading achievement, eventually their reading ability levels will plateau due to lack of exposure to higher-level texts.

Thomas states that students' listening comprehension sets the upper limits for reading comprehension (2011). This implies that students who are only exposed to texts that they can successfully read on their own will be limited in their comprehension. On the other hand, if we stretch students' comprehension levels upward through instructional read-aloud, their listening comprehension levels will impact the rate at which their reading comprehension levels increase. It is clear: *all* students will benefit from the instruction provided during read-aloud. We must ensure that *all* students remain in the classroom for this demanding work.

Certainly, students will need support as they rise to the challenge of this literacy-rich read-aloud content. *All* students, whether they are reading below, at, or above grade level, will need scaffolding as they encounter complicated texts. This is where the supports of guided practice will become important.

Working with an Instructional Read-Aloud Framework

Instructional read-aloud involves reading text aloud to students, thus relieving them of the challenging tasks of decoding and reading fluently. The teacher models fluent reading and also stops to share the cognitive processes used to comprehend the text. Each student is guided through this comprehension work through discussion, typically with a turn and talk partner. The instructional read-aloud levels the playing field for all students, allowing everyone the opportunity to participate in rigorous work.

Unlike the reading aloud done for fun after recess, instructional read-aloud provides explicit instruction in the process of reading and engages all students. Despite the hard work involved, students still label this as the "fun part of the day."

Explicit teaching within the instructional read-aloud is of vital importance, and the C. I. A. approach therefore follows a research-proven framework that includes:

- Connecting learning to past learning.

- Teaching and modeling specific reading skills.
- Providing the opportunity for guided practice.
- Linking the learning to daily reading habits.

The gradual release model is embedded in the instructional read-aloud framework in a way that allows students to gain knowledge and practice before trying on strategies independently (Calkins, 2001).

The instructional read-aloud helps all students achieve grade-level standards as they practice strategies, identify and use grade-level vocabulary, and rehearse grade-level standards in texts that are at or above their grade levels. The students' cognitive capacities are stretched as they access the background knowledge required of more difficult texts, and their reading stamina increases.

A read-aloud can be easily transformed into shared reading by giving students their own copies of the text being read aloud by the teacher. This shift in instructional theory allows students to use specific text evidence during partner talk and in written responses, which is a skill required of most of our students by the Common Core State Standards (CCSSI, 2010).

Instructional Read-Aloud Framework

STRATEGY:	BOOK:
Learning Target/Standard:	
Connection:	Yesterday we were working on…
Teaching:	Today I'm going to teach you…
Modeling:	Watch me as I model how I… While I'm reading, I want you to pay attention to how I…
Model #1	
Guided Practice:	Turn and Talk #1
	Turn and Talk #2
Link:	Today and every day I want you to…

Vocabulary

Explicit instruction in key vocabulary embedded in the instructional read-aloud text is a critical component of our work. Research indicates that the teacher read-aloud provides a major opportunity for students to learn new words (Cunningham & Allington, 2007). Not only is this focus on vocabulary essential for comprehension, it also facilitates vocabulary acquisition (NICHHD, 2000). Teaching key vocabulary prior to the reading of the text reduces the cognitive weight of the text. In the C. I. A. approach, key vocabulary is taught in mini-lessons that immediately precede the read-aloud.

The chart below offers a recommended routine for vocabulary instruction that focuses on teaching key repeated words and word contrasts that, together, will reveal an author's message. In this routine, a graphic organizer is paired with explicit instruction that focuses on structural analysis, context clues, and synonyms and antonyms of the word being studied (Appendix). Students connect this vocabulary to their own lives using nonlinguistic representations. Vocabulary will be further addressed in chapter 4.

Vocabulary Mini-Lesson Routine

1. Introduce the word and high-light morphemes.	*Today our target word is…* *If applicable:* *What is the root?* *What is the prefix? What does the prefix mean?* *What is the suffix? What does the suffix mean?*
2. Read the context(s) of the word. Highlight any clues that will help the reader infer the meaning.	*Our target word comes right from our text on page _____. Let's read it together. Are there any clues in the sentence that help us infer what this word means?*
3. Turn and talk: What does the word _____ mean?	*Based on the clues, what words or phrases describe this word? Turn and talk.*
4. Share-out and add to chart.	*What did you come up with?* *add accurate examples to the chart
5. Brainstorm other contexts for this word.	*In what other contexts might we find this word?* *add accurate examples to the chart
6. Turn and talk: What are opposites of this word?	*What words or phrases describe the opposite of this word? Turn and talk.*
7. Share-out and add to chart.	*What did you come up with?* *add accurate examples to the chart

8. I will remember this word…	*How will you remember this word? Draw a picture, or write a phrase that will help you remember this word. Use an example from your own life if possible.*
9. Link…	*Today and every day I want you to be looking for forms of this word in your reading. I also want you to practice using this word in your talk and in your writing.*

Oral Practice through Turn and Talk

Throughout the read-aloud experience, students will engage in expressive language through turn and talk. This discussion between partners allows for oral rehearsal of higher-level thinking skills and increases the level of engagement in classrooms. One of the best practices in the teaching of reading is that of giving students daily opportunities to talk in partnerships about their reading (Zemelman, Daniels, & Hyde, 2005).

Effective turn and talk engages students in conversations that lead to the expansion of ideas through debate (Schmoker, 2011). A deliberate structure for sharing and responding will encourage students to undertake this type of reciprocal dialogue. If designed and taught well, this structure will lift the level of talk, challenging students to use grade-level academic and content vocabulary.

A Talk Routine

I have always been very successful at helping teachers launch turn and talk in their classrooms. However, when faced with a classroom of my own fifth-graders, I struggled to move beyond the initial implementation of talk toward more thoughtful, literate discussions.

When I listened in on my partnerships, I routinely heard silence as students struggled to get started. Those that began their talk right away typically engaged in low-level conversations that rarely were supported by specific text evidence.

Hearing a partner respond to the other partner's thinking was an uncommon event that typically required my prompting. I struggled to determine the best way to engage my students in the level of talk I knew they were capable of. I needed a routine that I could use with my students that would be authentic, one that mimicked the back and forth sharing of ideas found in real-life conversations.

I turned to my sister and professional coach, Bethany Robinson, for advice. Her background in oral language development prompted us to implement a talk routine that uses stems to ignite and deepen conversation.

Turn and Talk Routine

Partner #1 *Share*	Shares thinking using a turn and talk stem: When the book said _____ I was thinking _____ because _____.
Partner #2 *Respond*	Responds to the partner's thinking using one of the following turn and talk stems: I agree/disagree with you because _____. I am also thinking _____. It sounds like you're saying _____.

Turn and Talk Stems

Turn and talk stems set up a deliberate structure for thoughtful conversations around literature. These stems help students get started on their thinking, and give them models of what sophisticated conversations sound like. Through our own modeling of the stems during think-aloud, teachers explicitly teach students how to participate in turn and talk conversations. These stems provide a scaffold for the sophisticated work of talking and, later, writing.

A successful turn and talk stem for fifth grade will hold students accountable for:

- Stopping to talk about their thinking at a critical place in the text.
- Naming what is important in a section of the text.
- Extending their thinking beyond the text.
- Citing evidence to support their thinking.

By carefully considering the expectations for comprehension work at each grade level, a variety of stems can be created to support students' thinking.

Turn and Talk Stems

STRATEGIES	
Connect	When the book said _____ I made a connection. I thought about _____. This helps me understand _____.
Visualize	When the book said _____ I visualized _____. This helps me understand _____.
Predict	When the book said _____ I made a prediction. I think _____ because _____.
Infer	When the book said _____ I inferred _____ because _____. This makes me think _____.
Determine Importance	When the book said _____ I thought this was important because _____. This makes me think _____.

Turn and Talk Stems

SKILLS	
Cause	When the book said _____ I was thinking it might have been caused by _____ because_____.
Effect	When the book said _____ I was thinking this might affect _____ by_____.
Compare	One important way _____ and _____ are alike is_____. This makes me think _____.
Contrast	One important difference between _____and _____ is_____. This makes me think_____.
Main Idea	When the book said _____ I was thinking the main idea of this section is _____ because_____.
Opinion	When the book said _____ I was thinking this shows the author's opinion. I think the author's opinion is _____ because _____.
Problem / Prediction	When the book said _____ I thought the main problem in the story was_____. I predict the problem might be solved by _____ because _____.
Solution / Opinion	In this story, the main problem is_____. The character's plan for solving the problem is_____. I think this is a good/bad solution to the problem because _____.
Drawing Conclusions	After reading _____ and _____ I am concluding _____ because _____.

Turn and Talk Stems

LITERARY ANALYSIS	
Author's Craft	When I read _____ I noticed the author_____. I think the author wants me to _____.
Empathy / Sympathy	When the book said _____ I felt empathy/sympathy for _____. I felt _____ because _____. This is helping me understand _____.
Mood	When the book said _____ I thought the mood was _____ because _____. This makes me think _____.
Theme	When the book said _____ I was thinking the theme of the book might be _____ because _____.
Generalizations	When the book said _____ I think the author was trying to tell me that _____ in general _____. This helps me think _____.
Foreshadowing	When I read _____ I thought the author was using foreshadowing. I think the author wants me to predict _____ because _____.
Turning Point	When the book said _____ I thought this was the turning point because _____. This makes me think _____.
Author's Message	When the book said _____ I thought the author's message was _____ because _____.
Evaluating the Author's Message	When the book said _____ I thought the author's message was _____ because _____. I agree/disagree because _____.

The stems given above will help students to get started during turn and talk. However, conversation is not each person sharing his or her ideas in turn, but the bouncing of ideas back and forth (Angelillo, 2003). To support students' practice of reciprocal conversations, response stems are also important. When responding, partners select one of the following stems:

- I agree/disagree with you because _____.
- I also think ____.
- It sounds like you are saying ____.

Planning for Turn and Talk

Not only will turn and talk support English language learners and struggling readers, it will also lift readers at the highest levels to a new standard of conversation. Angelillo tells us, "we must teach [students] how to talk about books and give them visions of what they can actually say" (2003, p. 18). Using talk routines and stems communicates how readers talk to one another authentically and trains students for this rigorous work.

To prepare for using the stems, create a poster that lists turn and talk partners. The more confident, higher-level reader in each partnership should be listed in the first column, and the less confident, more struggling reader should be listed in the second column. Ensure that each column is written in a different color. Initially, the students listed on the chart in the first column will be the starters, and students listed in the second column will be the responders. Roles will switch throughout the lesson; the struggling readers will always have a chance to hear their partners model the use of the stems before they are asked to take their turns.

Note: If you have an uneven number of students, create one trio. Place the student who is repeatedly absent or tardy in the trio. This will alleviate the stress of having to accommodate for that student's absences. Train students to join up with nearby partnerships when their regular partners are absent. This adjustment should be something students are responsible for on their own.

The turn and talk poster should be prominently displayed in your meeting area, to remind students who they are responsible for sitting with and what their roles in the partnerships will be.

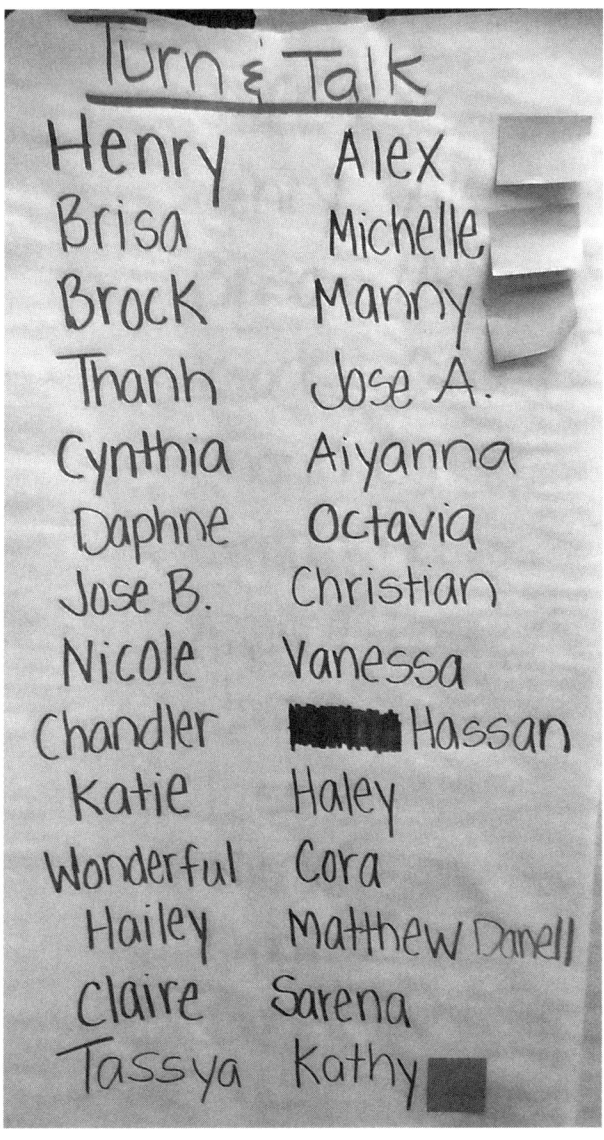

Sample turn and talk poster. Names in the left column are written in red. Names in the right column are written in blue. Sticky notes indicate which partnerships are assigned to the benches this week.

You will need a few materials to get you started using turn and talk stems:

- sentence strips
- a standard sentence-strip pocket chart
- markers
- clothespins or magnets in two colors
- a list of stems for the chosen unit of study
- a storage box for holding sentence strips

To prepare for turn and talk, follow the steps below.

1. Write all of the turn and talk starter and response stems that you will be using on sentence strips.
2. Display these stems in your pocket chart and hang the chart in the meeting area.
3. Use clothespins or magnets to indicate which turn and talk partner is sharing or responding.
4. Store additional sentence strips in the storage box. Store this box in your meeting area for ready use.

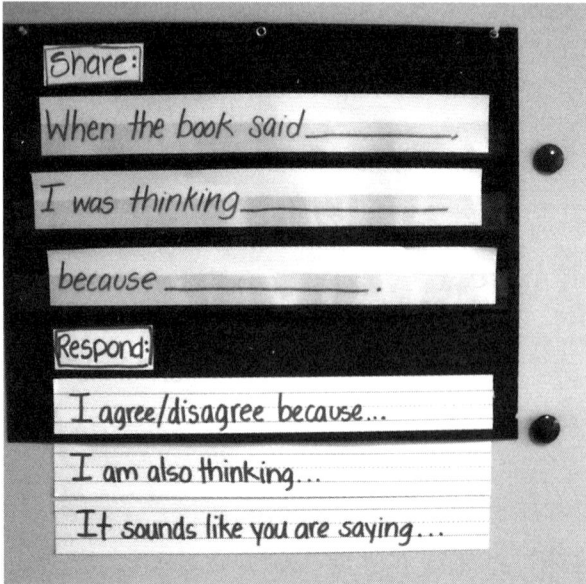

Sample stems chart with colored magnets to assign roles.

Encouraging Authentic Practices

The C. I. A. approach aims to promote practices that are authentic to the work of expert readers.

Layered Strategy Work

Research supports using combinations of reading strategies to improve reading comprehension, rather than teaching strategies in isolation. Therefore, as you design lessons or units, begin by considering how a combination of strategies can work together to achieve one single purpose.

For example, when reading *The Castle in the Attic* (Winthrop, 1985), students visualize the fantastical world described in the book and sketch a setting map using clues from the text. The closer to the villain's castle, the more parched the land becomes and the darker the surroundings. As students visualize this setting, they begin to compare and contrast the land near William's castle to the land near the villain's castle. They draw conclusions about the effects of evil on the environment. Over the course of three lessons, students access a variety of strategies for the purpose of developing higher-order thinking skills.

Throughout such layered strategy work, teachers must explicitly model the what, where, and why of strategy use. Teachers help low-achieving students become strategic readers by explicitly modeling the strategies and by teaching the value of applying them (NICHHD, 2000).

In the lessons for *The Castle in the Attic* described above, students are taught that good readers use clues in the story to help them visualize the setting. Good readers use visualizations to help them compare and contrast more than one setting. Good readers use evidence in the text to draw conclusions. Good readers use conclusions drawn from the text to consider a larger theme. Good readers note evidence in the text that supports a theme, in order to name the author's message. Good readers evaluate the author's message and determine how the author's message will apply to their lives.

Each lesson builds upon the lesson before it, with the ultimate goal of achieving proficient comprehension so that the text can be applied to one's life. This proficiency comes from using combined sets of strategies, a technique much more effective than applying strategies alone (Shanahan, 2011).

Layers of Comprehension Work

STRATEGIES	SKILLS	LITERARY ANALYSIS
Ask Questions	• Monitor and clarify • Identify the author's purpose	• Evaluate the author's purpose. Was the author effective?
Form Mental Images	• Describe the physical traits of a character • Describe the setting of a story • Notice literary devices	• Evaluate the author's craft • Distinguish between sympathy and empathy • Notice how the author creates mood
Determine Importance	• Identify the main idea and details • Identify the story sequence • Notice text features • Retell the important events • Identify the speaker/narrator • Explain why the setting is important to the story • Notice text organization • Find evidence of the author's purpose • Distinguish between fact and opinion	• Evaluate the author's craft. Did the author use organization effectively? • Draw conclusions • Make text-to-world connections • Analyze how one plot informs another (within a single text) • Determine the theme and support with text evidence

Make Text-to-Self Connections	• Activate background knowledge	• Make generalizations • Identify how an author makes a story/character believable • Recognize conflict: person vs. person, person vs. nature, person vs. self
Predict	• Cite evidence to support a prediction • Identify the story sequence • Identify a problem/solution • Identify cause and effect	• Recognize foreshadowing • Identify the turning point • Evaluate the solution
Infer	• Cite evidence to support an inference	• Make generalizations • Interpret implied meaning, e.g., metaphor, symbolism • Analyze how characters change over time
Synthesize	• Summarize • Compare and contrast • Formulate a personal response • Draw conclusions • Evaluate the author's effectiveness • Generalize	• Evaluate the author's effectiveness • Formally write in response to reading • Persuade • Make connections across texts • Apply to your life

Written Practice

Throughout the instructional read-aloud, students will receive models of sophisticated oral and written responses to text. Writing in response to reading will be used for a variety of purposes, with each type of written work being explicitly taught through modeled and guided writing.

Our written responses to reading typically serve one or more of the following purposes:
- to organize thinking
- to monitor thinking
- to expand thinking
- to synthesize thinking
- to reflect on thinking

As students are given opportunities to practice different types of writing, frames will help them get started and will help to organize and lift their thinking. Suggested frames will be shared in chapter 4.

Reader's Notebooks

Just as writers keep notebooks to record ideas for writing, readers keep notebooks to record thoughts while reading (Buckner, 2009). Like the co-created charts displayed in the meeting area, the reader's notebook will be a tool for comprehension.

I like to use the traditional composition books for student notebooks because they are durable, a nice size, and easy to make more personal. Students will need ample space in which to record information during read-aloud. They will also need pages for longer, informal writing. I recommend reserving approximately twenty pages for each read-aloud book, by using durable tabs to divide the pages in the notebooks into sections. If the tabs are put in ahead of time, students can enter work on more than one book at a time without worrying about running out of pages in any one section.

Students can personalize each notebook by adding clip art, magazine clippings, personal artwork, and stickers to the front and back cover. Cover the decorations with clear packing tape for durability.

A readers' notebook with tabs.   *A personalized composition book.*

Teaching with the End in Mind

To teach well, we must teach with the end in mind. I believe all students deserve to leave our K–12 education system prepared to continue their learning through college and beyond. This is certainly the goal expressed by the Common Core State Standards, which call for us to prepare students to proficiently read the complex text found in both college and careers (CCSSI, 2010). Therefore, we are all accountable for this work, and it must begin by a purposeful implementation of our priority: to reach *all* students through research-based practices that lift students to their highest achievement levels.

C. I. A. Overview

My mother is a puzzle lover. If you don't know what to get my mom for Christmas, you are always safe with a puzzle, as long as it is 500 pieces—no more, no less. I have memories from very early in my childhood of watching her set up the green card table in our TV room and begin her puzzle-a-thon. It always began the same way, with her carefully studying the cover of the box, glasses perched on the tip of her nose.

She had a definite ritual to her puzzle building. After studying the cover, she would carefully prop it up in the corner of the table, where it would be referred to frequently. Then, she began the tedious task of sorting all the pieces into orderly little stacks. This alone took my mother a good thirty minutes, and I remember wondering how she could have such patience to sort each piece before ever starting the puzzle. Finally, she would lay four obvious pieces on the table—the corners.

With the four corners in place, my mother quickly connected them by completing the frame. This task was efficiently managed by acquiring the noticeable edge pieces. With the frame in place, it finally looked like my mom was getting somewhere with her project. Already she had sacrificed an hour of the evening for this puzzle!

The fascinating part came next, when my mother would work not on the big picture but on placing patterns together. She would work on putting together the pale blue pieces or the pieces with red and white stripes. All across the table, the organized piles were put together like little miniature puzzles, which would then get attached to the frame. From the frame in, my mother's puzzle began to take shape. I watched as she worked more quickly now, laying the pieces in place almost effortlessly.

After hours of work, the puzzle was nearly complete, with only a few obvious pieces missing. She easily placed these last pieces and then proudly looked at the whole puzzle, an expression of satisfaction on her face.

Read As If You're Putting Together a Puzzle

Think of reading a book as being similar to putting together a puzzle (Arthur, 1994). Initially, the task—whether it involves a 500-piece puzzle or a 500-page book—may seem overwhelming simply because of its size. What do you do to overcome this sobering feeling? You break the task down so that it is made up of smaller tasks, just like my mother's puzzle ritual is. First, you study the box cover in order to understand what the outcome will be. For readers, the box cover is the book jacket. From the blurb on the back and clues on the cover, readers acquire critical information that they can use to infer genre and make predictions about the book.

Next, locating the obvious four corners helps the puzzle lover get something down on the table to build off of. For readers, identifying the most obvious information in the text—the characters, setting, problem, and main events—serves a comparable purpose. With this critical information in place, readers can then begin to develop their thinking around these main story elements.

Locate the four corners: character, setting, problem, and main events.

After laying down the four corners, puzzle builders sort out all the pieces with an edge and begin to connect the corners by building the frame. Readers will accomplish much the same thing as they begin to think about how the story elements relate to one another. For example, they might consider how the setting impacts the character, or how the character's traits influence the problem in the story.

Connect the corners by building the frame.
What's important for this genre?

With the frame complete, the next undertaking involves getting the puzzle to take shape, starting with obvious patterns. While puzzle lovers will begin to look for like colors and designs, readers will look for repeated words and ideas within the text, as these form patterns that will help readers perceive the bigger picture or the theme.

Use patterns to help you see the bigger picture.

Near the end, it is obvious how the puzzle will turn out. For readers, this is when the message the author wants them to take away from the book becomes clear. It is easy to lay the final pieces, and you finish with a sense of accomplishment and pride! This sense of satisfaction is what propels you to pick up another puzzle or book in order to recreate that feeling.

Know the author's message and quickly finish the book.

For students such as Damon who are struggling to gain the stamina to read longer chapter books, the puzzle analogy helps. Goals can be set that are accomplishable, and the purpose is clear.

The C. I. A. Model

The acronym C. I. A. stands for collect, interpret, and apply. Each word describes a critical stage of thinking outlined by the puzzle analogy. The C. I. A. approach is designed to help readers overcome the feeling of being overwhelmed that they have as they begin reading longer texts. It is also meant to increase students' understanding of complex texts, by helping them see patterns in the texts that will point them to authors' messages or themes.

The Four Stages of the C. I. A. Approach

I first arrived at the acronym C. I. A. while pursuing a goal of highlighting how the reading process should take readers up Bloom's Taxonomy (Bloom, 1956). Collecting critical information in order to gain basic knowledge and acquire low-level comprehension falls into the initial cognitive stage of Bloom's. This first stage is fundamental; without the critical knowledge acquired during this stage readers cannot get to the deeper thinking of application and analysis.

Interpretation comes next, as readers think more deeply about the text; they make connections within and across texts and consider larger concepts such as cause and effect, and compare and contrast. In the interpretation stage of reading, inferential thinking is at the heart of what readers do. While the acronym doesn't communicate this clearly, there are actually four stages to the C. I. A. approach, with interpretation being two-part.

The final level of Bloom's Taxonomy is synthesis and evaluation, which corresponds naturally to the work readers do as they finish books and begin to apply the books to their lives. At this stage, readers not only confirm the author's message, but also evaluate the message before thinking about how it will impact their own lives.

THE C. I. A. PROCESS	BLOOM'S TAXONOMY (BLOOM, 1956)
Collect Critical Information	Knowledge & Comprehension
Interpret the text	Application & Analysis
Apply to your life	Synthesis & Evaluation

The stages of C. I. A. help readers, such as Alex, who struggle to know what type of thinking to engage in throughout a longer text. In addition to outlining higher thinking processes, the acronym is engaging for students. They get excited about becoming C. I. A. members, and this membership plays a major role in our classroom community.

Fifth-grade boys proudly hold up their C. I. A. membership cards.

The C. I. A. work begins with selection of a text and division of that text into four relatively equal parts. Students simply use sticky notes to flag the quadrants in their books. The text can be of any genre that follows a narrative sequence, and it can also be of any length. However, the purpose is to make longer text manageable for students, so chapter books are what I will refer to throughout this discussion.

This copy of Holes *(Sachar, 1998) shows quadrants marked by sticky notes.*

Timing

One significant aspect of the C. I. A. process is the timing of each stage. As in the puzzle analogy, the first part of the work is time-consuming, but eventually the work speed increases, allowing for more enjoyment of the book. In the beginning, as readers collect critical information, the work is laborious. Much of the students' thinking will be written down, and they will reread the text several times as necessary. Yet, as readers move through each stage, the pace gradually increases. Eventually, readers should be able to read the last chunk of the book without interruption.

When I think about the natural rhythms of my own reading, this pattern makes sense. As I start a new piece of literature, I read slowly and often reread to make sure I have the important elements in my head. I even find myself returning to the blurb. Because I am a seasoned reader, I do not let this arduous work overwhelm me; I know that my pace will quicken and my enjoyment of the book will increase once I get past this first part.

Eventually, I near the end of the book. This is when I tell my husband and children not to bother me for the next hour because I am finishing a book and do not, under any circumstances, want to be interrupted! I look forward to this stage in my reading the most, and when I am done, I am usually disappointed that the story has ended. It is this pure enjoyment that I experience on completion of a book that propels me to select and read another. If our students don't have the opportunity to experience this joy and satisfaction, we can never hope to engage them as lifelong readers.

C Collect critical information	**I** Interpret the text		**A** Apply to your life
During this quadrant of the text readers • Name the important **characters** and infer character traits. • Name and visualize the **setting.** • Think about the **problem** and **important events.** • Use comprehension strategies to **monitor** comprehension.	**During this quadrant of the text readers** • Use comprehension strategies to get to **deeper thinking.** • Recognize key **repeated words/ phrases.** • Start to think about possible **lines of thinking.**	**During this quadrant of the text readers** • Look for **evidence** to support a line of thinking.	**During this quadrant of the text readers** • Continue to look for **evidence** to support a line of thinking. • Confirm and revise **predictions.** • Think about **problems/solutions/ results.** • **Evaluate** how the author ties up all the loose ends. • Consider how the book will impact their **lives.**
Readers read **slowly** and often **reread.**	Readers **increase their speed** a little bit, and reread less.	Readers **increase their speed** even more and rarely, if ever, reread.	Readers **read without interruption** to the end.
At the end of the first quarter, readers **stop and summarize** in order to check comprehension and make sure they have the story in their heads.	At the end of the 2nd quarter, readers **stop and name a line of thinking.**	At the end of the 3rd quarter, readers find the **turning point and** consider how the turning point reveals the **author's message.** Here, readers **predict** how the book will end.	At the end of the book, readers **confirm or reject their predictions** and **evaluate** the author's ending. Then readers reflect on their reading by summarizing and synthesizing the text. Finally, they evaluate the author's message.

The Joy in Completion

At the end of one school year, I met informally with my principal in her office. She began by complimenting me on how much reading my students had engaged in over the course of the school year. She told me that not only had she observed this, she had also had a conversation with a parent of one of my students out in the parking lot. The parent was telling my principal how happy she was that her daughter had read so many chapter books during the year. The parent went on to say that, in all her life, she herself had never finished reading a book.

As my principal was telling me this, tears filled her eyes. We both sat in silence as we pondered the story. What would it be like to live without the joy of reading a book to its end? Neither one of us could even imagine it.

The intrinsic value of reading that is revealed to us when we finish a book is the only reward that will carry our students into lifelong reading. I cannot stress enough how urgent this work is.

Teaching from the Heart

One of my favorite professional authors is Katie Wood Ray. I think I enjoy her professional books for teachers so much because I relate to her pedagogy. She believes that our teaching must be "driven by what we know…as a *reader* and *writer*, not as a teacher" (2002, p. xiii). So in understanding and developing this C. I. A. process, I began by looking at what *I* do as a reader and making that explicit for my students.

For too long, I allowed myself to teach reading practices that were not authentic to the work *I* do as a reader. How could I expect my students to joyfully and willingly participate in these practices if they couldn't see the purpose of the practices? How could I expect students to transfer an activity into their own reading lives if it had to be adjusted to accommodate the real reading world?

The process I outline for my students in the C. I. A. model is drawn from my own experiences as a reader. My students know this because I share with them how the process helps me in my own reading life.

I "get real" with them as we try on C. I. A. strategies. They see them as lifelong reading habits that they will continue to use outside our classroom walls.

By midyear, it will be common to see students stapling packets of paper together to make their own reader's notebooks. When I saw one of my students, Wonderful, doing this in January, I asked her what she was up to. She responded, "Oh. I'm making a reader's notebook. Aiyanna, Tassya, and I are starting our own book club!"

It is when the students in my classroom surprise me like this that I quickly grab my conference notecards and write these moments down as evidence that C. I. A. habits have transferred into my students' personal reading lives. After all, the true evidence of our work is seen in our students' lifelong reading engagement.

Collecting Critical Information in Quadrant 1:
Identifying the Main Story Elements

My bedside table is stacked with books. The stack has grown so big that it has now spread to cover both the nightstand and the entire surrounding floor. At a glance, it would look like I am an avid reader, completing several books within a week. In fact, my life is so busy with professional reading, I hardly have the time for the novels loaned or gifted to me by family and friends. Many of the novels that sit beside my bed have been started and quickly abandoned.

I am supposed to be an expert reader, and yet I find myself in the same cycle as my students. Why? Because starting a new book demands focus, determination, and stamina. Starting a new book requires a certain level of concentration and dedication that I simply do not have at ten o'clock at night, when I finally settle under the covers to read. Before I am even three pages in, my eyelids begin to drop and the dream I begin to have somehow weaves its way into the plot of the story. Sound familiar?

Beginning to read a book requires purposeful work. In the early pages of a chapter book, readers must interrogate the text through observation. They must look for the critical information the story is built around: character, setting, problem, and main events. Like the four corner pieces of a puzzle, these story elements will be the most easily identifiable pieces of the text. However, organizing the information in one's mind can be a challenge, especially for newly fluent readers who are reading stories with multiple plots, problems, and/or themes. The truth is, beginning a book is more often than not a slow and challenging process. This reality must be explicitly shared with our students. Otherwise, we run the risk of implying that reading is easy, and thereby defeating our students before they even get started.

Reading during the first quadrant of a text does not have to be a defeating process. If we teach students key strategies and processes for collecting critical information early in a book, they will have the foundational pieces necessary for success in the remaining quadrants.

Using the Blurb to Get Started

I am always surprised at how many of my students pick a book and begin reading it without ever reading the blurb. When I ask why they don't read the blurb before reading, some of them say they don't read the blurb because they don't want to spoil the book by knowing what will happen. I smile and say, "Have you ever put together a puzzle without looking at the lid? When you put together a puzzle, it is pretty important to first know what the picture is supposed to look like. Have you ever looked at the lid, put together the puzzle, and then been disappointed to find that the puzzle looks just like the picture? Of course not! When the puzzle matches the picture, you are happy that you put it together right!"

I encourage students to think about reading the same way. The blurb on the back of the book tells us how the story will go, and helps us get the story in our heads before we start reading the first chapters. While we read, if we have confusion, sometimes rereading the blurb helps us improve our comprehension. The blurb is essential for helping us picture the story in our minds before we start to read the book and for checking our understanding as we go.

I rely on the blurb to guide my conferences with students. Most of the books they are reading during independent reading are books I have not read myself. When I first started conferring with students, I quickly learned that reading the blurbs on the backs of their books gives me enough information to support my students in conferences. Clearly, this is a strategy that can also help my students as they begin new books. The blurb provides supports that they need as they begin reading.

Character, Setting, Plot

I now ask students to use the blurb before reading the text, to help them identify the critical information needed to get the story in their heads: character, setting, and plot. Then, as they begin to read the book, they continue to gather information or clues about these three main story elements.

The blurb becomes the source of information for the first critical entry in the reader's notebook (Appendix). It is where students begin to identify the essential information that they collect during the first stage in the C. I. A. approach.

Out of the
Dust

Out of the Dust by Karen Hesse (Blurb)

A terrible accident has transformed Billie Jo's life, scarring her inside and out. Her mother is gone. Her father can't talk about it. And the one things that might make her feel better – playing the piano – is impossible with her wounded hands.

To make matters worse, dust storms are devastating the family farm and all the farms nearby. While others flee from the dust bowl, Billie Jo is left to find peace in the bleak landscape of Oklahoma – and in the surprising landscape of her own heart.

Characters: Billie Jo, Mother (gone) father
likes playing piano

Setting (place): Panhandle, on a farm, Oklahoma

Setting (time): 1934, winter,

Problem: terrible accident, Billie Jo's hands are wounded.

Questions: Why is Billie Jo staying in Oklahoma? How did all these terrible accidents happen?

Predictions: I predict Billie Jo will find the "Peace".

Student notebook entry for the blurb of Out of the Dust
(Hesse, 1999).

Inferring Genre

As they read the blurb, along with gathering critical information, readers will also pay close attention to vocabulary that alludes to the genre and theme of the book. The more students understand genre, the easier it will be for them to infer genre from the language used in the blurb.

Within the blurb for the book *Out of the Dust* (Hesse, 1999), readers might notice references to inner peace, and to how Billie Jo transforms after overcoming devastating hardships, in the line "Billie Jo is left to find peace in the bleak landscape of Oklahoma—and in the surprising landscape of her own heart." Readers will more quickly identify the significance of this reference if they know enough about the genre of the book, which in this case is historical fiction.

Understanding Genre

Complex text can be made more comfortable and predictable for students as we explicitly teach the nuances of genre. This predictability is easy to identify when we focus on what we can expect of character, setting, and plot within a single genre. Brilliantly, student exposure to the predictability of various genres will increase their enjoyment of challenging text.

To better explain this, we will look at what we can expect from character, setting, and plot within the general categories of realistic fiction, fantasy, and narrative nonfiction.

Realistic Fiction

Realistic fiction is exactly what the title states: realistic. It is a story with a narrative flow that is made up, yet very believable. Subgenres within realistic fiction include adventure, mystery, and historical fiction. While each of these subgenres has unique traits, there are commonalities across the broader category.

Readers of realistic fiction can expect to find characters who seem very real and who remind them of people they know in their own lives. Sometimes, readers will even see themselves in the characters. Just as the characters are believable, so is the setting. While reading realistic fiction, readers will be thinking about how the main character changes over time. This is a key element of the plot that will reveal the author's message.

REALISTIC FICTION	
Setting	Realistic/believable place Present time
Characters	Made-up characters that are very real and believable The main character changes over time.
Plot	The character must deal with a real-life problem. The character changes over time.

Fantasy

Fantasy refers to the use of one's imagination. Therefore, fantasy stories will always include elements of make-believe. The emphasis of fantastical elements is dependent upon the type of fantasy. Subgenres include, but are not limited to, talking animals and epic fantasy.

As in realistic fiction, readers can expect to see a change in the main character over time. Focusing on this change will help readers recognize the author's message. Typical of the fantasy genre is the concept of the "unexpected hero." Throughout the story, the main character will prove to be heroic through brave accomplishments.

The setting will always have elements of fantasy, with some settings being entirely fantastical and others being somewhat fantastical. In all fantasy stories there will be elements of good and bad, and right and wrong. Therefore, this tension typically drives the plot.

FANTASY	

Setting	Fantastical setting
	  • Real world, fantastical elements
	  • Fantastical world, real-world elements
	Time is relatively unimportant or nonexistent.

Characters	Real or fantastical Good vs. bad, hero vs. villain The main character changes over time (unexpected hero revealed).
Plot	Tension between good and bad, right and wrong

Narrative Nonfiction

Narrative nonfiction is nonfiction text that is written to tell a story; therefore, elements of character, setting, and plot can be identified within the text. Examples of subgenres of narrative nonfiction include biography, autobiography, and historical nonfiction.

When reading narrative nonfiction, readers can expect the characters, setting, and plot to be real. The author will reveal "key players": people the author believes are important to know about. In addition, the author will share information to help readers draw conclusions about groups of people. Readers consider how the setting and the events in the peoples' lives impact who they become.

NARRATIVE NONFICTION	
Setting	Real place Real time (present or past)
Characters	Key players (important people the author thinks we should know about) Groups of people
Plot	The characters deal with a real-life problem (current or historical event). The characters are changed by the setting and events.

Understanding genre and its predictable elements helps readers determine what is important to write down or pay attention to during the collecting phase and supports their future attempts to interpret the text. With the genre inferred, readers are ready to move into the text and begin collecting critical information from the first quadrant.

Collecting Critical Information

Just as puzzle lovers look for the obvious corner pieces first, readers look for the most obvious information as they begin to read a chapter book. What the author thinks is most important to the story will be most obvious in the text. At the beginning of a book, the most obviously important information will be about the characters, setting, and plot. Therefore, readers should be paying attention to and gathering information about these elements.

When readers start a new book, they are reading with the purpose of "figuring it out"; they are working to determine characters, setting, and plot, as well as to gain a basic understanding of how the book is going to go. At the beginning of a book, readers typically have thoughts on every page. They take careful notice of story elements, begin to infer about the main characters, ask an assortment of questions, and make predictions. All of their insights will seem important enough to write down, to the point that readers will feel as though their thoughts are taking them away from the pure enjoyment of the book. However, by writing critical information down, readers set themselves up for understanding; they lay the groundwork for deeper thinking.

This laborious and, sometimes, tedious work of collecting will be most pronounced in the first quadrant. At this stage, readers will not only take copious notes, they will also reread the text to gain meaning. I often read the first chapter or two of every book twice, as I skim pages for character names or plot shifts, trying to make sense of this new and challenging text. While this act of reading is time-consuming, it is the work of expert readers. We do an injustice to our students when we let them believe that reading comprehension comes naturally to good readers.

Tackling the Qualitative Demands of Complex Text

One of my favorite books of all time is *Holes*, written by Louis Sachar (1998). Every time I read this book I pick up on subtleties within the layered plots that I had not noticed before. It is Sachar's satirical writing style, manipulation of time sequence, use of irony and metaphor, and implicit representation of biblical themes that make this book enjoyable and challenging even for sophisticated readers. While quantitatively this book is at a third-grade Lexile level, qualitatively it stretches the reading ability levels of students in fifth and sixth grade.

The qualitative demands of texts at higher levels include:
- Multiple meaning levels
- Implicit themes (multiple themes)
- Complex structures (events not in chronological order)
- Sophisticated vocabulary
- Figurative language
- Multiple perspectives
- Increased intertextuality

In addition, an increase in content knowledge, literary knowledge, and cultural knowledge is required to recognize themes, perspectives, nuances of language, and ambiguous references to other texts.

Our challenge, as outlined in the Common Core State Standards (CCSSI, 2010), is to help readers navigate the complex nuances of text within the complexity band appointed for each grade level. This requires teaching specific strategies for reading sophisticated text that will be transferable into independent reading.

Perhaps the most authentic strategy we can teach is the habit of highlighting or noting important information while reading, for the purpose of monitoring comprehension and checking understanding. This note-taking strategy acts as a tool for organizing thinking while reading, making it easier to move toward higher-level thinking.

When we introduce students to the many ways in which readers collect their thinking while reading, we give them the opportunity to make choices. If students are allowed to try out the various ways in which readers collect thinking, they will begin to engage in the authentic work of readers. They will learn to collect as a way of organizing their thinking, and they will see collection as a comprehension tool, not a reading activity. Helping students understand the purpose for our collections begins with modeling.

Collecting strategies are initially taught during the read-aloud, when students and teacher are creating charts together. To more fully engage in this practice, students copy these charts into their reader's notebooks. Later, the charts will provide examples for students to follow as they transfer these strategies into their own reading, either in partnerships or independently.

Collecting Characters

Keeping track of a myriad of characters in complex texts such as *Holes* (Sachar, 1998) and *Walk Two Moons* (Creech, 1994) can be a challenge that overwhelms and deflates our students. Therefore, the second entry in the reader's notebook is usually a basic list of the important characters. This list will serve as a reference as readers face obstacles in the book. Character traits stated or implied in the book can be added for additional reference.

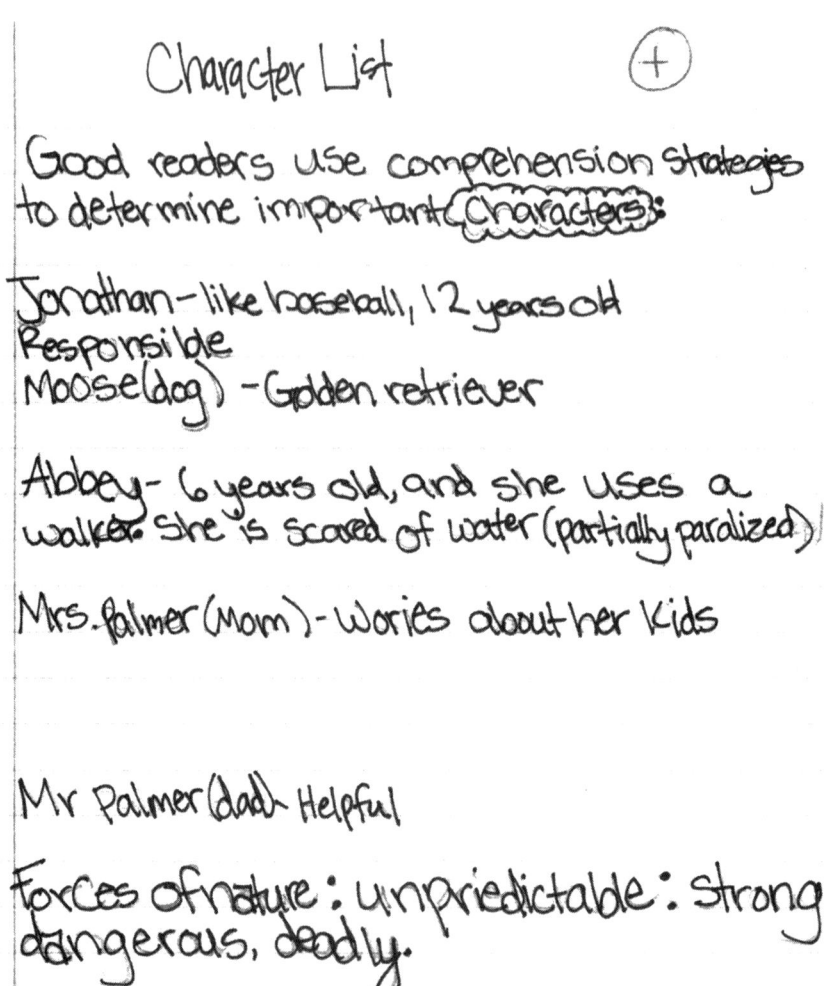

Character List $(+)$

Good readers use comprehension strategies to determine important (Characters):

Jonathan - like baseball, 12 years old
Responsible
Moose (dog) - Golden retriever

Abbey - 6 years old, and she uses a walker. She is scared of water (partially paralized)

Mrs. Palmer (Mom) - Worries about her kids

Mr Palmer (dad) - Helpful

Forces of nature: unpriedictable: strong dangerous, deadly.

Character list for Earthquake Terror *(Kehret, 1996).*

As text complexity increases, it may become important to implement other strategies for collecting characters. In the book *Holes* (1998), Sachar's multidimensional story line requires readers to keep track of the main character's place in the family tree. In *this* case, a family tree that is used to keep track of generations of characters becomes a critical entry in the notebook.

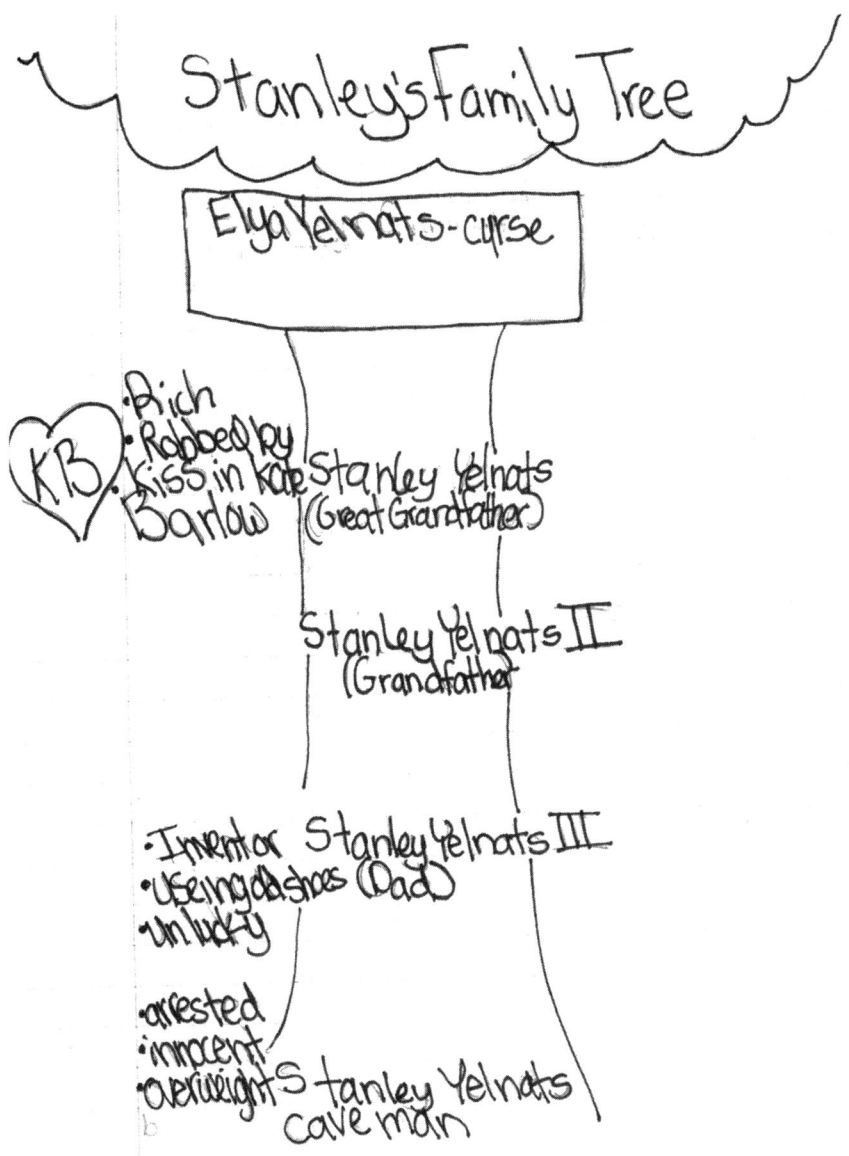

Family tree entry for Holes *(Sachar, 1998).*

In this same book, Sachar layers three separate plots, each with its own set of characters. When collecting character names in this text, readers will need to organize these characters into separate lists, distinguished by each plot title. Keeping these separate lists helps readers not only to delineate these unique plots, but also to draw conclusions as to their distinctive similarities.

In complex texts, readers must draw upon their background knowledge in order to understand characters better. When reading *The Castle in the Attic* (Winthrop, 1985), it is helpful for readers to sketch the character of the Silver Knight in their notebooks in order to draw upon their knowledge of medieval knights. Sometimes, readers bring misconceptions or stereotypes to a book, and sketching can draw out these misconstructions.

In the book *Holes* (1998), Sachar deliberately references the Warden in the first part of the book, without ever revealing clues as to her physical appearance. Students typically visualize a tall, strong male in a professional uniform, gun on hip. Later, they must revise this visualization when they learn that the Warden, in fact, is a redheaded female who has long, red fingernails and wears cowboy boots. Revisions to thinking show advanced thinking skills, and this advanced thinking will be required of students reading complex texts.

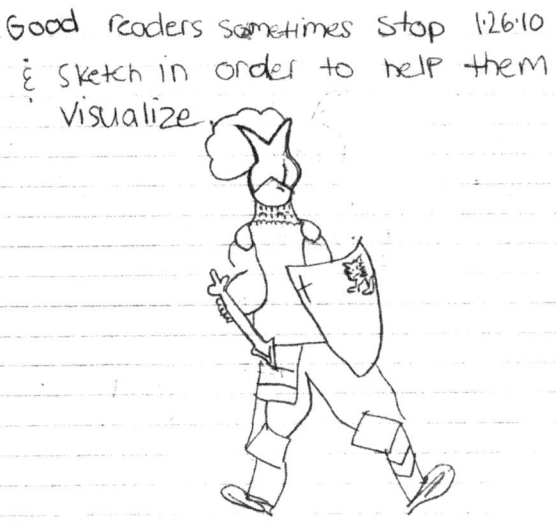

Sketch of the Silver Knight from The Castle in the Attic *(Winthrop, 1985).*

A student's visualization of the Warden from Holes *(Sachar, 1998).*

Keeping Track of the Setting

The setting is an important element that tests and defines characters. In genres such as historical fiction, science fiction, and historical nonfiction, the setting is critical to the plot. In all genres, it will be important for readers to note the setting, including both time and place. In complex text, these details about the setting are generally less obvious than other elements in the text and therefore must be inferred.

Maps are ideal tools for keeping track of where a story takes place, and they can be very helpful to readers. In addition to helping students keep track of setting clues, maps can be created and then revised after further reading, to note changes in the setting over time. While reading *Earthquake Terror* (Kehret, 1996), readers sketch the setting of the story, Magpie Island, based on clues in the text. Throughout the reading of this book they revise the map, noting the impact of the earthquake on the environment. Through this collection, students gain a greater understanding of cause and effect.

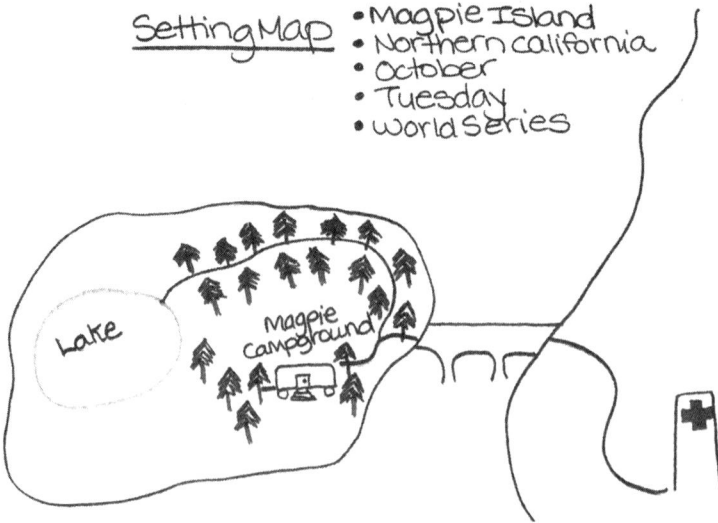

Setting maps are used to keep track of important setting clues and to help readers visualize. This map of Magpie Island was drawn in the early stages of reading the book Earthquake Terror *(Kehret, 1996) and then revised after further reading.*

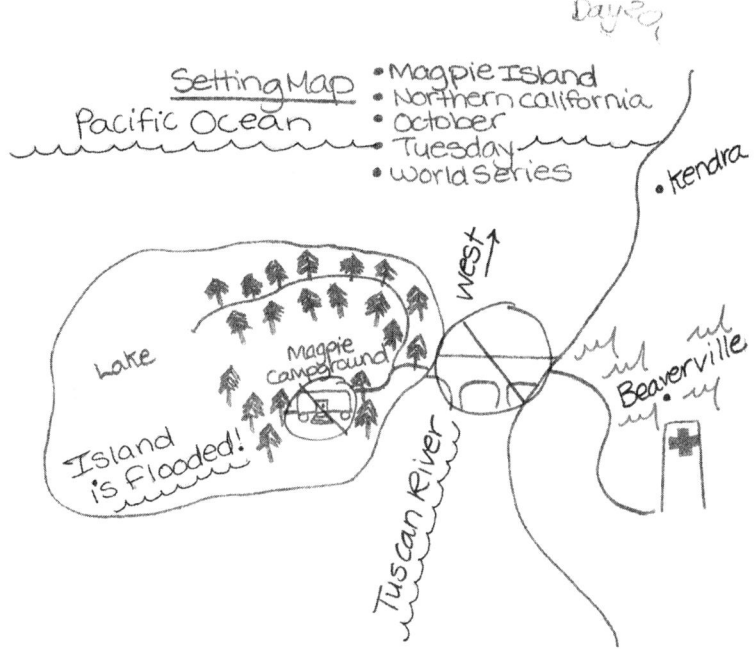

This revised setting map shows the effects of the earthquake on the environment.

When the location of the story is a real place, as in historical and realistic texts, it is helpful for students to identify this location on a map. Doing so helps them see where the story takes place in relation to the larger world. When reading *Earthquake Terror* (Kehret, 1996), readers use a map of California that shows the San Andreas Fault to infer where Magpie Island might be located. When reading *Children of the Dust Bowl* (Stanley, 1992), readers keep track of the migration route of the Okies during the Great Depression, using a map of the United States to make predictions about the hardships the Okies will face on their journey.

Students infer where Magpie Island is located on a California map.

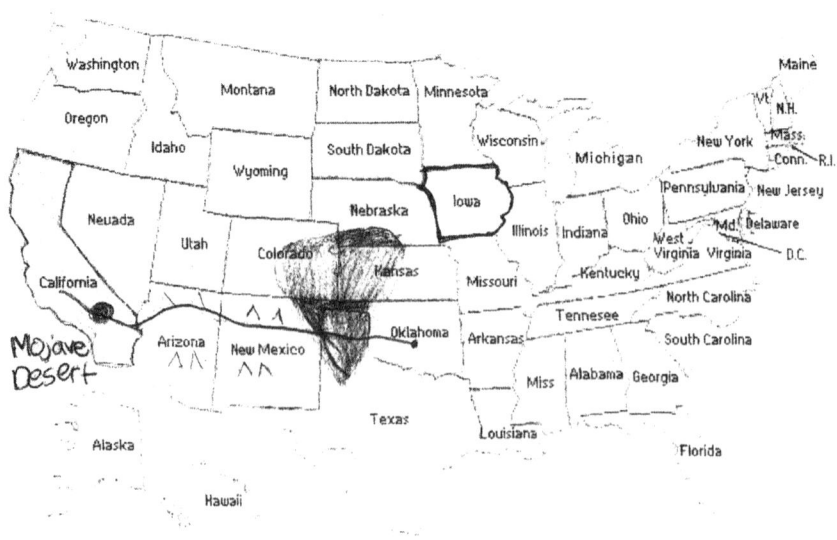

Students map the migration route of the Okies during the Great Depression.

Following the Plot

From my observations, I've learned that, in general, the most difficult element of text for students to process is the plot, which requires them to sift through events and details to determine which are most important. As texts increase in complexity, readers will be challenged to keep track of more than one plot and to consider how these parallel plots support each other. This challenge is often overpowering, and may cause students to give up and abandon text. We can break this cycle by indoctrinating strategies for determining importance.

First, readers must keep track of important events while reading, and they must keep these events in chronological order. In chapter books, there are typically one to two main events introduced per chapter. While reading the first quadrant of the book, it may be necessary for students to keep a paraphrased list of these main events. In addition, students will name the big problem(s) in the book.

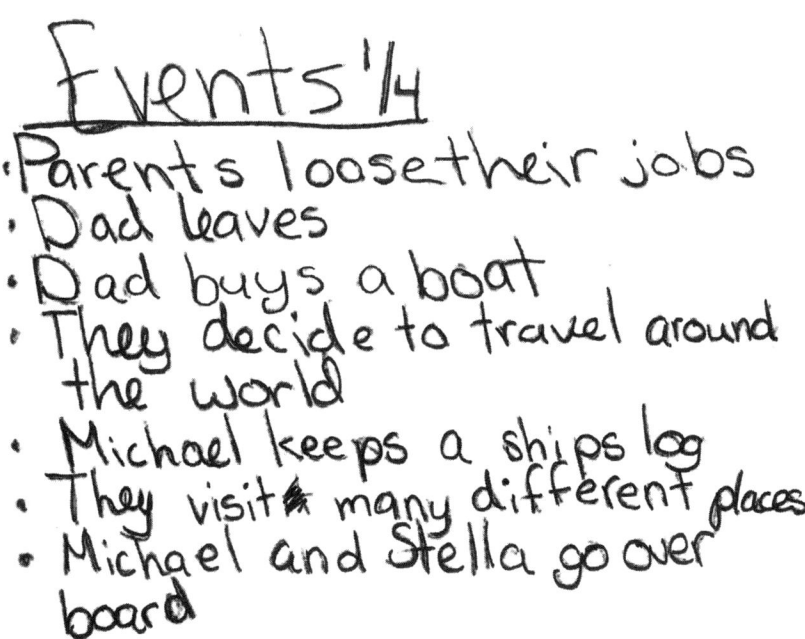

Readers keep track of important events in the first quadrant of
Kensuke's Kingdom *(Morpurgo, 2003).*

Plot:

Problem: The city is falling apart. They are running out of supplies. (lightbulbs) The generator breaks down all the time and no one knows how it works.

Readers stop to name the big problem revealed in the first quadrant of The City of Ember *(DuPrau, 2003).*

Stories with multiple plots will be more complex. When students are reading stories with multiple plots, such as *Walk Two Moons* (Creech, 1994), I recommend that they keep lists of the different plots, and of events within those plots. Also, students can use colored flags or sticky notes to mark shifts in the plot, while reading.

Complex Story Structure

Main Plot: Driving to Idaho
Sal, Gramps & Gran

(pink flag)

Sub Plot #1: Phoebe's Story

(blue flag)

Sub Plot #2: Sal's memories of her mother

(yellow flag)

Readers keep track of multiple plots in Walk Two Moons *(Creech, 1994).*

This copy of Walk Two Moons *(Creech, 1994)
has been marked with colored flags to show the
shifting of multiple plots.*

Timelines can be particularly helpful when reading books with an unconventional structure. For example, when reading *Maniac Magee* (Spinelli, 1990) and *The City of Ember* (DuPrau, 2003), which have plots with large gaps, timelines can help distinguish these gaps and engage readers in inferential thinking.

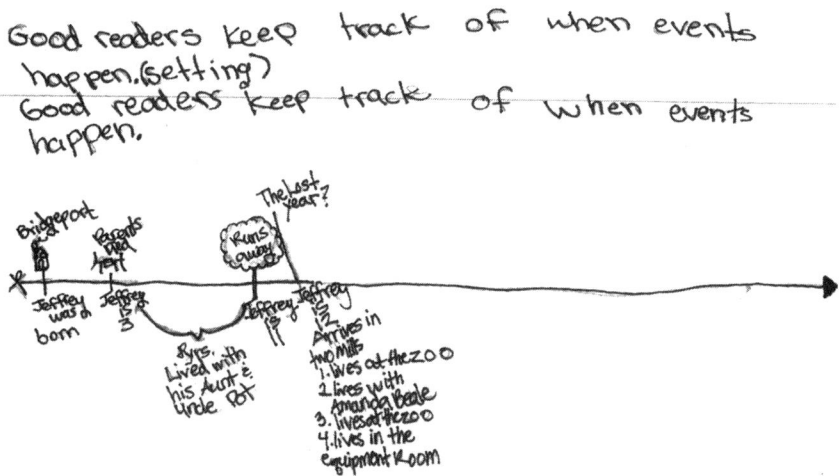

Timeline of events in Maniac Magee *(Spinelli, 1990).*

Timelines can also help readers access background knowledge about a time in history. When reading *Children of the Dustbowl* (Stanley, 1992), it may be helpful for readers to place important events on a historical timeline that includes surrounding events from history. This helps readers place a book within a larger time span.

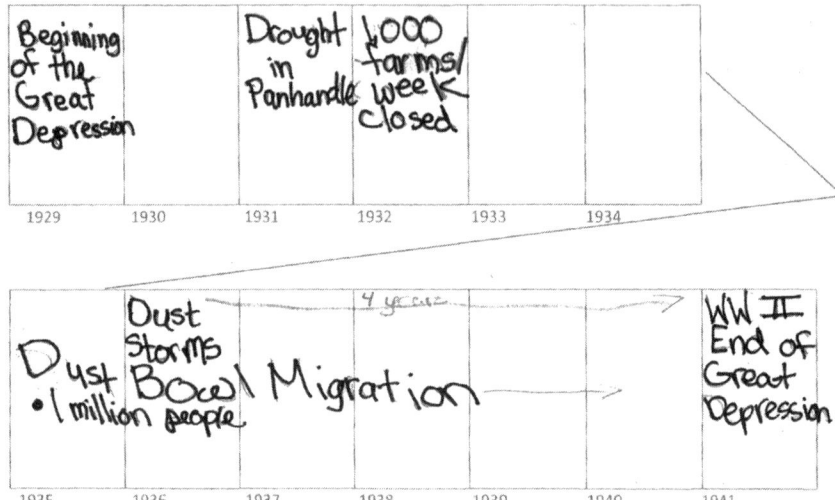

Timeline of events surrounding the Dust Bowl Migration.

Summarizing, the First Check-Stop

Misconceptions acquired in the first quadrant of the text must be described and corrected before readers engage in the work of interpretation that begins in the second quadrant of text. Therefore, it is critical that readers stop after reading the first quadrant and summarize the text for the purpose of monitoring comprehension. A retell summary requires students to generally state what the first quadrant of the text is about and to then expand on that by elaborating on the main events or ideas from this section of the text. Finally, a concluding statement moves students toward bigger thinking as they share predictions or conclusions drawn from this first section of the text.

While serving as a tool for comprehension, the retell summary also provides an opportunity to teach the expectations of quality writing. Supporting student writers with a retell summary frame will help them gain skills for organizing and lifting their levels of writing to more mature levels. Frames are meant to transition students quickly from modeling and guided practice to independence in writing.

Retell Summary Frame (Quadrant 1)

Introduction Sentence	*The first one-fourth of the book* _____, *by* _____, *tells/explains* _____ _____.
Body	Describe the most important events from this section of the text. Use transition words such as: *First, next, then, finally,* *First, next, after that, in the end,* *In the beginning, then, after that, finally,*
Conclusion	Describe your thinking about the book. This could be a prediction about what will happen next, an inference about the theme, or a judgment. Use concluding words such as: *In conclusion,* *All in all,* *As you can see,* *It is true,* *I am thinking,*

Adapted from Step Up to Writing *(Auman, 2010)*

(+)

Summary

The first four chapters of <u>Earthquake Terror</u> by Peg Kehret tells about a disasterous earthquake. In the beginning Jonathan's family is camping on Magpie Island when Mrs. Palmer breaks her ankle. Mr. Palmer took Mrs. Palmer to the hospital leaving Jonathan taking care of Abby and Moose. Jonathan, Moose and Abby started to hike to their camper when Moose acted strange. Jonathan heard rumbling noise. The ground started to shake. The word flashed accrossed Jonathan's brain. "Earthquake!" Jonathan said getting low to the ground. Jonathan grabbed Abby and layed under a tree fallen under another tree leaving a gap. When the earthquake ended, Abby's walker has been broken. Jonathan lead Abby to the trail. Jonathan felt a rumble. He and Abby got to the ground. It was an aftershock.

Clearly earthquakes are really bad disasters to be in I wouldn't want to be in this dangerous disaster!

Retell summary of the first quadrant of Earthquake Terror *(Kehret, 1996).*

Assessing the First Quadrant

The C. I. A. model provides teachers many opportunities to practice ongoing informal assessment. This is described as assessment *for* learning, which "happens while learning is still underway. These are the assessments we conduct throughout teaching and learning to diagnose student needs, plan our next steps in instruction, provide students with feedback they can use to improve the quality of their work..." (Stiggins, Arter, Chappuis, & Chappuis, 2006, p. 31).

Listening in on Turn and Talk

One of the key ways teachers will gather information for learning is by listening in on student dialogue during turn and talk. In this scenario, teachers will primarily be listening for how well students use the opportunity to talk with a partner to process thinking. In addition, teachers will check for students' understanding of how to use strategy work to support comprehension.

Taking notes on partner conversations can be easily done using a grid (Appendix) attached to a clipboard. Record student names in order of partnerships, mimicking the color coding you have used on the turn and talk poster. This way, you will always know who is responsible for sharing and who is responsible for responding. During turn and talk, purposefully listen in on partnerships. Do this by carefully walking through the meeting area and getting down close as students talk. Always remain in the role of an observer or coach, never taking over the conversation or doing the students' work for them.

Keep your notes focused on the *kind* of talk students are engaged in.

- Is the talk reciprocal?
- Is the starter prepared with thinking?
- Does the starter use the stem to practice key vocabulary and to support thinking with textual evidence?
- Does the responder practice active listening?
- Does the responder thoughtfully respond using textual evidence?
- Does this reciprocal conversation demonstrate that students have met the learning target for listening comprehension?

Checking Reader's Notebooks

In the first quadrant, notebook entries will be used to name critical information. When looking at student charts, you will be checking for understanding and will be helping students with misconceptions improve their comprehension. I want students to know that the work of the first quadrant is messy, sometimes imperfect, and must be revised as readers reread or acquire new information. Therefore, early charts in the reader's notebooks are not assigned a formal grade. Instead, I look to see if students are keeping their charts well organized and easy to read. If these charts are going to be used as tools throughout the reading of the rest of the book, they must be legible and easy to find. Stickers and smiley faces motivate students and encourage neat work, even in fifth grade.

Formal grading of summaries at the end of the first quadrant will give teachers the opportunity to record scores for their grade-books. In those notebook entries, teachers see evidence of how well each student has collected critical information and synthesized that information into a written summary.

When scoring short writing pieces in the reader's notebooks, such as the retell summaries, I wander the room, grading student work as I go. Having the students alongside me as I grade their work gives them the opportunity to self-evaluate. In addition, students are allowed to make changes to their work with my guidance. I simply mark in the margin whether the work was completed independently or with my support. Through the use of this scoring practice (Schmoker, 2011), students receive immediate feedback on their work, are guided in their progress, and take ownership in their learning. In addition, I no longer give student notebooks rides in my car! Because I grade fewer papers at night I am less overwhelmed. I'm therefore motivated to assign more opportunities for writing practice; my students are completing far more written assignments than before.

Retell - Summary (Determine Importance)

Nice job! Well organized. Could be a little shorter.

Interventional	Instructional	Independent	Advanced
• Summary does not tell only the most important events. • May be missing key events from the beginning, middle or end. • May include incorrect information	• Includes more than the most important events from the beginning, middle and end • May not clearly state the problem • May not clearly state the resolution	• Includes most important events from the beginning, middle and end • Tells the main problem in the book • Tells how the problem was resolved • May include more details than necessary	• Clearly written, well organized summary • Includes the most important events from the beginning, middle and end • Tells the main problem in the book • Tells how the problem was resolved • Paraphrased in no more than 6 sentences

An example of a summary rubric, filled out by the teacher and student and then taped into the reader's notebook.

Cementing the Foundations

This work of collecting critical information in the first quadrant of text may seem tedious and time-consuming, but it is foundational to the comprehension of the text as a whole. Many times, text is misinterpreted when steps in this critical stage are omitted. Accurate interpretation can only take place after essential information about characters, setting, and plot has been collected and understood. Arthur writes, "If you rush into interpretation without laying the vital foundation of observation, your understanding becomes colored by your own presuppositions—what *you* think, what *you* feel, or what *other people* have said" (Arthur, 1994, p. 25). When we fail to take time for the critical work of collecting, the message of the book becomes distorted by our inaccurate thought processes.

As I write this, I am reminded of a student, VJ, who was often misdirected by his own creative thinking. I remember all too well his contributions to a book club studying the novel *Because of Winn Dixie*, by Kate DiCamillo (2000). Despite obvious clues in the text that indicated otherwise, VJ's prediction was that one of the characters in the book, Miss Franny Block (who is quite old, by the way) was actually Opal's mother, and that by the end of the story Franny would reveal this to Opal and they would live happily ever after. To the rest of us in the book club, this prediction was absurd, and it took every ounce of our energy to convince VJ otherwise. Because VJ hadn't taken the time to carefully read the first quadrant of the text, his interpretations were clouded by his own premonitions.

The work of quadrant one is critical in laying a foundation of literal understanding. Here, we "give children tools for thinking [that] help them to think and read with new depth and a new sense of possibility" (Calkins, 2001, p. 385). These tools will support readers as they launch forward into the second and third quadrants, where they will experience a deepening of thought that promotes higher-level thinking.

Interpreting the Text in Quadrant 2:

Using Comprehension Strategies to Develop Deeper Thinking

Putting together a puzzle, for my mother, is a ritual. She follows methodical steps, working slowly at first. After laying the four corners she begins to build the outer frame, first separating out the pieces that are important to this process. Looking for patterns in the pieces—shape, color, design—my mother uses those patterns to simplify an otherwise difficult task.

Reading is like putting together a puzzle. When reading, readers move from identifying what is most obvious in the text, to identifying subtle patterns. The author's craft manifests in these elusive patterns, which all point to the author's intentional message. In the second quadrant, readers slow down, digging deeper in the text in order to identify themes.

Digging Deeper

Crossing over from the first quadrant of text into the second quadrant marks the shift from observing what is obvious in the text to noticing what is hidden or ambiguous. As readers navigate increasingly sophisticated levels of text, they will be challenged by corresponding increases in textual ambiguities. Therefore, strategies for reducing the cognitive weight of text will be needed to enable students to proficiently read text at these rising levels of complexity.

Strategies we can use to deepen students' understanding of text include:

- Intentionally exposing vocabulary and literary devices embedded in the text, to increase students' understanding of the author's craft.
- Providing opportunities for dialogue both in partnerships and larger groups.
- Engaging students in purposeful writing tasks that broaden their understanding of text.
- Explicitly teaching patterns of predictability in genres to promote a deeper understanding of relationships within and across texts.
- Nudging students toward a line of thinking or theme that will be supported by evidence revealed in the text.

Noticing Craft: Vocabulary and Literary Devices

Writers intentionally use their craft—their selection and organization of words—to convey the overall messages or themes of their books. Authors very deliberately select and place key repeated words throughout their writing, with the purpose of communicating a message. These repeated words are like a key; "they unlock the meaning of the text" (Arthur, 1994, p. 36).

Recognizing key repeated words in the text makes the implicit, explicit. Careful readers will become alarmingly aware of the author's purposeful craft.

Consider the following excerpt from *Walk Two Moons*:

Then one day at lunch, [Phoebe] slid into the seat next to me and said, "Sal, you're ever so <u>courageous</u>. You're ever so <u>brave</u>."

To tell you the truth, I was surprised. You could have knocked me over with a chicken feather.

"Me? I'm not <u>brave</u>," I said.

I was not. I, Salamanca Tree Hiddle, was afraid of lots and lots of things...What I have since realized is that if people expect you to be <u>brave</u>, sometimes you pretend you that you are, even when you are frightened down to your very bones. (Creech, 1994, p. 13–14, emphasis mine)

Early in her book, Creech emphasizes the word *brave* through repetition of this word and its synonyms. She continues to repeat the word *brave* throughout the book, using it at least seventeen times. It becomes quite clear that she wants the reader to focus on this term and to consider what it means to be courageous.

Selecting Mature Vocabulary

Mature vocabulary needed for proficient understanding of the text comprises the words that are most critical for students to know and understand in order to reach higher-level thinking. Because students engage in challenging, complex books during the instructional read-aloud, they will encounter many words that they do not know. Teachers will be tempted to teach them all, in the hopes of increasing students' comprehension. In fact, "narrowing the number of words you are going to teach to a reasonable number will increase the chances that all your children will learn them" (Cunningham & Allington, 2007, p. 98).

When selecting words to teach in explicit vocabulary lessons, focusing on key repeated words will not only support students' understanding of the theme but will also broaden their understanding of second-tier words—words that are frequently used across a variety of domains. Students are typically familiar with these second-tier words, and often bring a general understanding of these words to the text. Precise instruction on a second-tier word is intended to broaden the student's application of the word (Beck, McKeown & Kucan, 2002).

Vocabulary: Making Connections

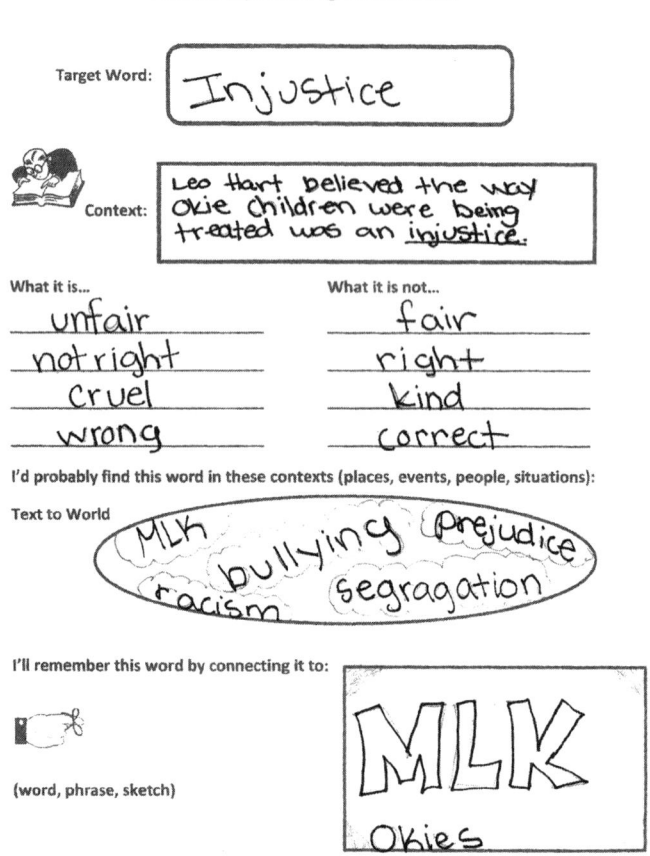

Target Word: Injustice

Context: Leo Hart believed the way Okie children were being treated was an injustice.

What it is...
- unfair
- not right
- cruel
- wrong

What it is not...
- fair
- right
- kind
- correct

I'd probably find this word in these contexts (places, events, people, situations):

Text to World
MLK bullying prejudice racism segragation

I'll remember this word by connecting it to:

(word, phrase, sketch)

MLK Okies

Entry in one student's vocabulary handbook for the word injustice, which repeats throughout the book Children of the Dust Bowl *(Stanley, 1992).*

Pre-teaching Inferred Words

Paying attention to patterns in inferential thinking will also unlock meaning for our students. Just as authors purposely include repetition of language, they also repeatedly draw the reader toward meaningful inferences. When working with students, we must teach these word-inferences in pre-taught vocabulary lessons, to ensure that students are able to use important inferred words at critical spots in the text.

My best example of this comes from the book *The Castle in the*

Attic, by Elizabeth Winthrop (1985). In the book, William does not want his nanny to leave. He decides he must come up with a way to get her to stay. When nothing else works, he uses a magical token to shrink her. Later, the reader infers that he regrets his actions. The word *regret* is one of the most important words for understanding the theme of good versus evil. Readers use the word *regret* to infer that even the hero in the story is not perfect. What separates the hero from the villain is the fact that the hero later regrets his or her bad choices.

Without this word, *regret*, in their vocabulary, readers would never be able to infer regret within the context of the story. While it is an essential word for understanding the theme, Elizabeth Winthrop never uses the word in the text.

When designing the unit of study for *The Castle in the Attic* (Winthrop 1985), I noted that the word *regret* would have to be taught prior to the moment when readers would need to infer it.

Highlighting Key Words and Contrasts

The author's interpretation of truth is revealed through key words and contrasts (Arthur, 1994). In the excerpt I shared earlier from *Walk Two Moons*, Creech not only directs our thoughts to what it means to be brave, but also defines the term through contrast. She differentiates the words *brave* and *frightened* by writing, "What I have since realized is that if people expect you to be brave, sometimes you pretend that you are, even when you are frightened down to your very bones" (1994, p. 14). This is not the only place in the text where she draws the reader's attention to this contrast. In fact, the word *frightened* and its synonyms repeat a total of twenty-six times throughout the text, with *brave* and *frightened* appearing together at least four times. What Creech reveals to the reader is that bravery has something to do with being frightened; bravery involves overcoming one's fears.

Without knowing to look for key repeated words and contrasts, readers could easily miss the messages that authors reveal through carefully chosen words and crafting.

Contrasts appear all throughout the book *Holes* (1998), as part of Sachar's sarcastic style. Early in the book, readers zero in on the concept of coincidence versus destiny. This concept captures the theme later revealed—that we all are given opportunities to change our destinies.

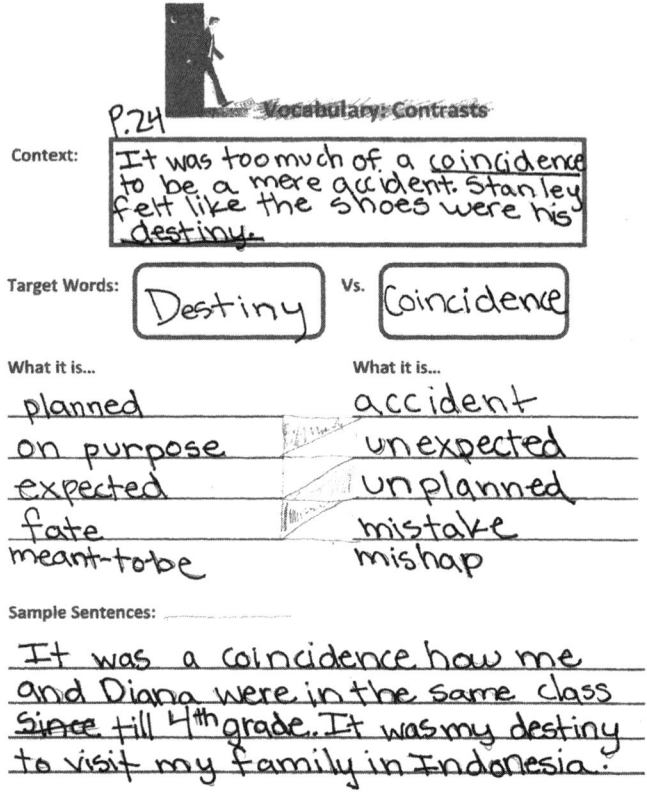

Entry in one student's vocabulary handbook showing the contrast between the words coincidence *and* destiny *in* Holes *(Sachar, 1998).*

Teaching Vocabulary that Increases Conceptual Understanding

When selecting repeated words to teach students, be guided by the principle that those words that point to the theme of the text or that develop an important concept will be worth spending time on. Knowledge of a word that students already know the meaning of will be expanded as they consider synonyms and antonyms of the word, as well as the use of the word in the larger context of the text.

In addition, the purpose of building students' vocabulary is not simply to give them the ability to define a "new" word. Teachers also want to help students recognize the wide use of the word being studied and learn how to apply it across a variety of contexts. The purpose, then, becomes to develop conceptual understanding so that students are able to provide "precision and specificity" when describing or using the word (Beck et al., 2002, p. 19).

When working with students on the book *The City of Ember* by Jeanne DuPrau (2003), I came across the word *trapped* in the book. While the word was one my students could already define, I knew that it would be important to activate their knowledge of the word in order to help them to fully understand the metaphor introduced in the following chapter. I decided to spend some time explicitly teaching the word *trapped* and its synonyms.

While students were working on the graphic organizer for the word *trapped*, they came up with the word *tyranny* as a synonym. I was shocked. They had voluntarily connected the word *trapped* to a previously learned vocabulary word, and in doing so they had broadened their understanding of both words. I knew that, despite my doubts, I had made the right choice to stop and spend time on this word. In addition, the students were better prepared for moving into the next day's lesson, in which they had to recognize the author's use of metaphor.

While it is necessary to make these types of judgment calls, what you do *not* want to do is stop to spend time on every single unknown word in the text. This will not only bog students down, it will also take away from the enjoyment of the book. Words that must be defined for students in order for them to understand a certain sentence or paragraph can be dealt with quickly by your provision of a definition or synonym of the word while you are reading. More information beyond this is usually not required.

While reading the book *Children of the Dust Bowl*, by Jerry Stanley (1992), aloud to my students, I came across the word *surplus*. I knew my students did not know the meaning of the word, so I simply addressed it for them as we read. The word was not a key word that pointed to the theme; therefore, this was the only attention I needed to give the word.

The following sample read-aloud script defines the word *surplus* quickly through teacher think-aloud:

Teacher Read-Aloud: "The farms often produced more than could be picked or sold, but if the Okies tried to help themselves to the surplus crop…"

Teacher Think-Aloud: or extra crop

Teacher Read-Aloud: "…left on the ground, the growers might pour oil on the food…" (Stanley, 1992, p. 26)

Reinforcing Vocabulary: Practice Makes Perfect

"When effective instruction is part of the classroom practice and students are encouraged to use the sophisticated words they are learning, they begin to take true ownership of the words" (Beck et al., 2002, p. 72). Ownership is fostered as students are given authentic opportunities to use the newly learned vocabulary in the context of rigorous classroom discussion and writing.

This is why I encourage teaching words before students see or use them in the text. If students know a word and then are given the opportunity to use the word immediately in their turn and talk, they will be more likely to understand and remember that word. If students are participating in informal or formal writing assignments, they have further authentic opportunities to practice the word. Students need multiple encounters with words before they become known (Beck et al., 2002).

Understanding the Author's Style

Style refers to the way the author writes and is also purposeful in directing the reader to the author's message. Picking up on the author's style is tricky, as readers must recognize literary devices including humor, irony, sarcasm, metaphor, symbolism, mood, and tone.

When reading *Holes* (1998), readers must note Sachar's sarcastic tone in order to pick up on his viewpoint. He writes, "If you take a bad boy and make him dig a hole every day in the hot sun, it will turn him into a good boy. That was what some people thought" (p. 5). Without noting the sarcastic tone, readers might assume that Sachar agrees that juvenile boot camps are helpful. In fact, the entire novel is written satirically, demonstrating Sachar's belief in the opposite.

In the second quadrant, it is important for readers to become aware of word choices and literary devices that the author uses to direct the reader toward the overall theme. By intentionally teaching students to slow down and notice these nuances of text, teachers empower them with the tools to interpret the text for themselves. In the second quadrant, the patterns within the text will be used as a starting point for developing high-level thinking. Charts made in the second quadrant will draw attention to the author's craft.

One student notes Rowling's use of humor in Harry Potter and the Sorcerer's Stone *(1997).*

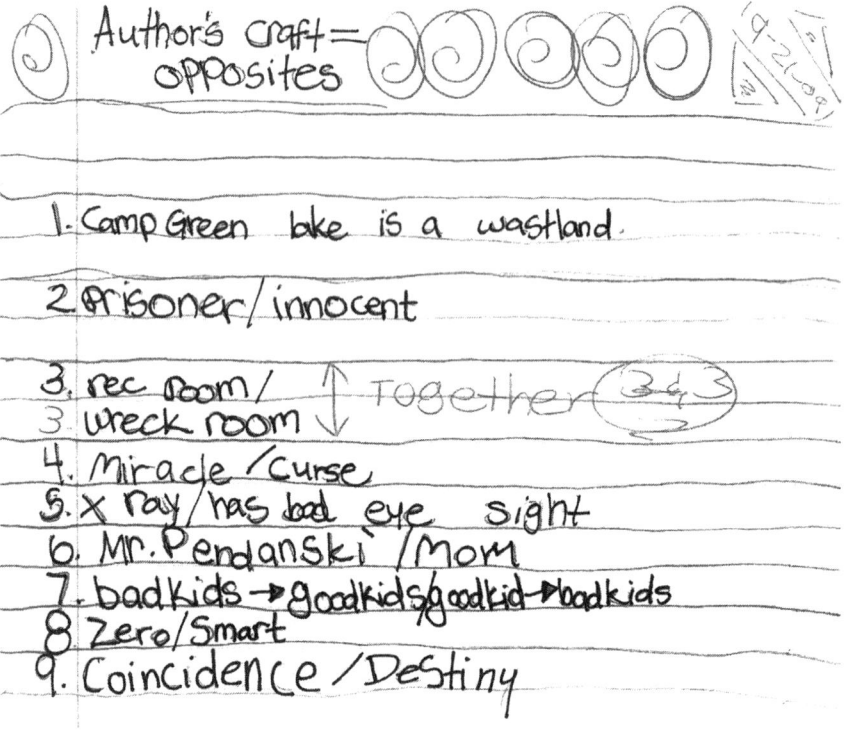

Author's craft = opposites

1. Camp Green lake is a wastland.

2. Prisoner / innocent

3. rec room /
3. wreck room   ↑↓ Together (3&3)

4. Miracle / Curse

5. X ray / has bad eye sight

6. Mr. Pendanski / Mom

7. bad kids → good kids / good kid → bad kids

8. Zero / Smart

9. Coincidence / Destiny

List of opposites (irony) in the book Holes *(Sachar, 1998).*

"Cut off a vine and it will grow back...
you must pull it out of the ground
and burn it to ensure it is dead."
(p.89)

Metaphor: The plant or vine is
a metaphor for the hope of
freedom.

Looking closely at the author's use of metaphor in the book Chains
(Anderson, 2008).

Symbolism

Good Readers look for the use of symbolism when they read in order to understand the author's message.

Description of "The Migrant Mother"
The picture of The Migrant Mother shows a woman who seems very sad. She must be migrating with her children. It looks like she's thinking as her children squeeze close to her.

good observation!

She is a symbol of:
Survival
hope
strength
courage
bravery
pride

★ I will remember the migrant mother as a symbol of strength when I feel hurt and hopeless and over whelmed.

yes!

One student's response to the use of symbolism in Children of the Dust Bowl *(Stanley, 1992).*

Using Dialoguing to Extend Thinking

Reading actively requires having an internal conversation with text. When readers make this conversation external through talk, they have the opportunity to extend their thinking in collaboration with others. Ideas build on each other, as partners add to or disagree with each other's thinking. Setting up turn and talk partnerships and giving students a framework for talk supports them as they use conversations to pull out their deep thinking.

In the following turn and talk conversation, you will see how one student's thinking ignites the other student's thinking. Their conversation describes the book *The City of Ember* (DuPrau, 2003) and models how readers can use their knowledge of genre to help them figure out plot.

Student 1: When the book said that Sadge went into the unknown regions and came back saying that the rocks were sharp as nails and the rats were the size of houses I was thinking Sadge was exaggerating, because this book is science fiction and has to be believable.

Student 2: I disagree with you. I think Sadge was lying. I think he found something in the unknown regions that he doesn't want people to know about, so he is lying to keep people from going to the unknown regions. I think he is being greedy because I noticed there's always a greedy character in books.

In this conversation, talk stems and knowledge of the genre support the students' ability to use textual evidence to elaborate on their thinking. Partner response challenges thinking as Student 1 considers his partner's perspective. Explicitly teaching students how to have responsive conversations about text will move them toward the production of thoughtful written responses.

Using Writing to Extend Thinking

Taking notes while reading the first quadrant of the text looks different from the informal writing that students do as they read the second quadrant of the text. However, the work of the first quadrant supports the work of the second. While charting won't be eliminated, charting in the second quadrant is less frequent and more focused on what is essential for the genre.

During this stage, students expand their thinking by completing written stems and informal writing pieces. These pieces of writing support students as they access specific skills necessary for moving into higher-level thinking.

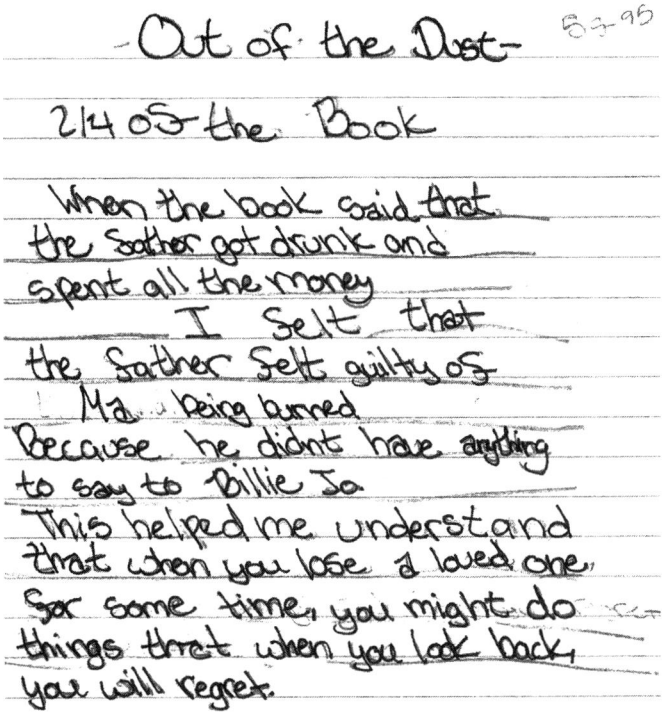

Stems are used in writing to lift student thinking.

Skills practiced in informal writing include describing cause and effect, comparing and contrasting, and identifying problems and solutions. In addition, students will begin to debate issues brought up in the text as they recognize the author's opinion or solution to the problem, and consider their own ideas and beliefs.

Cause and Effect

While reading *Children of the Dust Bowl* (Stanley, 1992), students write about the cause and effect relationships identified throughout the text. One student writes,

In the book *Children of the Dust Bowl* by Jerry Stanley, the dust storms in the Panhandle caused many other treacherous events to occur. The Okies had just gone through the terrible dust storms. Now, as a result of the dust storms, 1,000 farmers per week closed their farms down. After the farmers had lost their farms they were in desperate need of a job. They heard that in California there were many jobs available. Thousands of Okies traveled to California to find work. They thought California would be paradise, but the Okies didn't know that in California they didn't need that many workers. My prediction is that many of the Okies will go jobless. As a result of the dust storms, the Okies will be depressed and homeless.

By noticing cause and effect relationships in this text, students understand how events in history impact groups of people and change the course of lives. Students are challenged to think about how these events in history have significance in our world today.

Cause and Effect Frame

Introduction Sentence	_____ *caused* __ _____ _____. This sentence should tell the major event and also broadly tell the effect of this event.
Body	Describe several events that happened as a result of the one major event. Include **some** detail. Use transition words such as: *First, next, then, finally, First, next, after that, in the end, In the beginning, then, after that, finally,*
Conclusion	Describe your thinking about the book. This could be a prediction about what will happen next, an inference about the theme, or a judgment. Use concluding words such as: *In conclusion, All in all, As you can see, It is true, I am thinking, I predict,*

Adapted from Step Up to Writing *(Auman, 2010)*

Compare and Contrast

Identifying similarities and differences within a text prods read- ers toward drawing conclusions. When reading *Maniac Magee* (Spinelli, 1990), students notice similarities and differences between two characters in the text, Maniac and Grayson. As these similarities and differences are charted, students conclude that these characters, while different in age, are for the most part very similar. One student writes,

Maniac is a twelve-year-old boy and Grayson is an old man who is probably seventy years old but, for the most part, they are very similar. First, both Maniac and Grayson do not have families that they can rely on. They both ran away and live on their own. Second, Maniac and Grayson both think they are unlucky and choose to be solitary. Also, they are both good hearted and act like good Samaritans. Finally, they teach each other. Grayson teaches Maniac baseball and Maniac teaches Grayson to read. In conclusion, I think it doesn't matter how old you are, people of different ages can still be a lot alike.

Comparing and contrasting literary elements in a text helps students to draw conclusions within a text and to consider how those conclusions communicate a larger theme.

Compare/Contrast Frame

Introduction Sentence	If the two things are **more alike** than different, begin by saying: _____ is _____ and _____ is _____, *but for the most part they are similar.* If the two things are **more different** than alike, begin by saying: _____ and _____ both _____, *but overall they are very different.*
Body	Explain the ways these two things are either alike or different. Use transition words such as: *First, second, third,* *One way, another way, also,* *First, also, in addition,*
Conclusion	Restate your thinking. Start with one of the following phrases: *In conclusion,* *All in all,* *As you can see,* *It is true,* *To sum up,*

Adapted from Step Up to Writing *(Auman, 2010)*

Problem/Solution/Opinion

Critical literacy supports the idea that through reading and writing, students have the power to take a critical stance. To do so, readers must simultaneously acknowledge the author's perspective and avoid being manipulated by it (McLaughlin & DeVoogd, 2004). We can teach students to recognize the author's perspective and then form their own opinions. After reading several chapters of *Earthquake Terror* (Kehret, 1996), one student writes,

Jonathan's mother, Mrs. Palmer, breaks her ankle while they are camping on Magpie Island. Mr. Palmer decides to take Mrs. Palmer to town, leaving Jonathan and Abby alone on the island. I think this is a bad decision. First, like it said in the book, it would take them a long time to get to the trailer because Abby is partially paralyzed. Also, they have no equipment (the first aid kit is in the trailer). In addition, it said Jonathan didn't like to be alone, and on the island they are isolated. Jonathan and Abby will have to know how to survive because the island is primitive. In conclusion, I think Mr. and Mrs. Palmer should not have left Jonathan and Abby alone on the island. I predict the earthquake will happen while they are alone.

Within this writing piece, there is evidence of debate as the student not only forms her own opinion in response to the text, but uses text evidence to back up her thinking.

Problem/Solution/Opinion Frame

Introduction Sentences	State the problem and solution.
	Tell whether you agree or disagree with how the problem was solved.
Body	Give strong evidence that supports your opinion.
	(Evidence can come from the text and/or your own life.)
Conclusion	Restate your thinking.
	Start with one of the following phrases: *In conclusion, All in all, As you can see, It is true, To sum up,*

Adapted from Step Up to Writing *(Auman, 2010)*

Incorporating Outside Text

Helping students consider other perspectives involves researching topics in outside sources. When reading *Holes* (1998), students conclude that Louis Sachar does not believe in juvenile boot camps as a means of effective rehabilitation. His book communicates one side of the issue. To help students draw their own conclusions, it is important to bring in outside text for consideration. After reading articles that illustrate both the good and bad consequences of boot camps, students form their own opinions and support those opinions with evidence. One student writes,

I think juvenile boot camps are a bad option for troubled youth. One reason is because they have to participate in a lot of physical exercise. For some kids, this is unhealthy. One fourteen-year-old girl actually died of heart failure after running three miles. Another reason I think it is a bad idea is because some people who go to boot camps are actually innocent, like Stanley in the book *Holes*. Also, one boy was put in a juvenile boot camp just because he stole $25.00 from a friend. Lastly, when people get out of boot camp they can become even worse! For instance, I read that some people commit more serious crimes after boot camp. I thought that boot camps were supposed to make people better, not worse. In conclusion, I think it turns out that sometimes, juvenile boot camps don't work.

Introducing outside text in the second quadrant can help students draw conclusions and develop their own opinions. This research work supports critical literacy and challenges students to extend their thinking beyond the text.

Assessing Informal Writing in Quadrants 2–4

Informal writing will demonstrate the ability of students to use strategies and skills to get to deeper thinking. Therefore, students' informal writing in quadrants two through four will show evidence of their progress toward mastery of standards. When students begin their informal writing work, I like to have them place target stickers at the top of their notebook pages. The target stickers, which are simply red garage-sale dots topped with hole protectors, give students a visual reminder that they need to demonstrate on-grade-level work. Throughout the year, students can help create rubrics for grade-level writing expectations, which should be prominently posted in the room. Rubrics might be updated at the beginning of each trimester in order to show increased expectations.

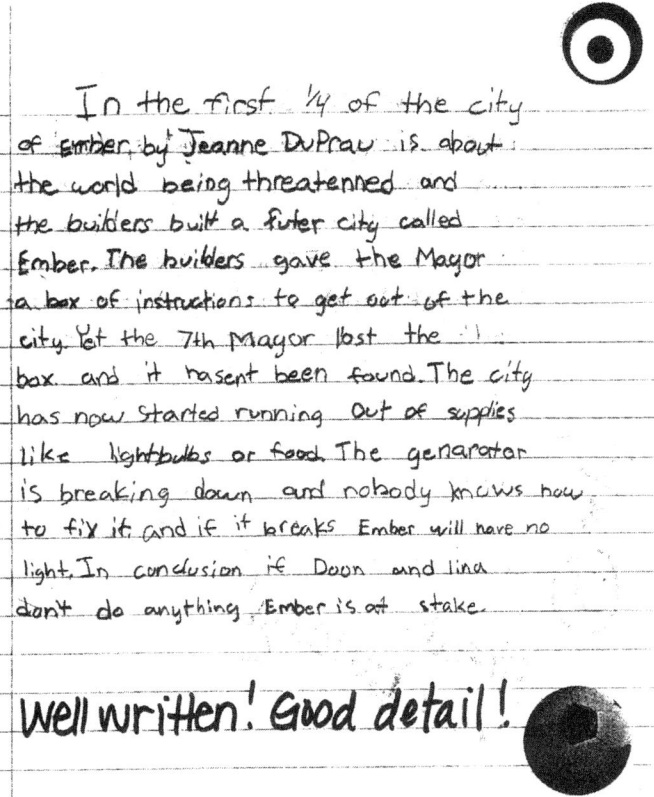

In the first 1/4 of the city
of Ember by Jeanne DuPrau is about
the world being threatenned and
the builders built a futer city called
Ember. The builders gave the Mayor
a box of instructions to get out of the
city. Yet the 7th Mayor lost the
box and it hasent been found. The city
has now started running out of supplies
like lightbulbs or food. The genarator
is breaking down and nobody knows how
to fix it and if it breaks Ember will have no
light. In conclusion if Doon and lina
don't do anything Ember is at stake.

Well written! Good detail!

*Students are reminded to produce grade-level writing by target
stickers placed at the top of pages in their notebooks.*

Again, when grading these informal writing pieces, I work *with* students. At the completion of a writing assignment, they know to leave their reader's notebooks open and to be ready to read their writing to me when I come to them. Together, each student and I will assess where the student is in mastering the targeted grade-level standards.

While grading student work, I also allow students the opportunity to revise their work with my guidance. Immediate feedback, and the opportunity to act on this feedback, has been proven to increase student success (Schmoker, 2011).

In addition to expecting students to meet rubric requirements, I also expect students to demonstrate the use of new vocabulary in their writing. It is exciting to see students taking risks with their word choices. Implementation of new words in their writing proves increased understanding (Beck et al., 2002).

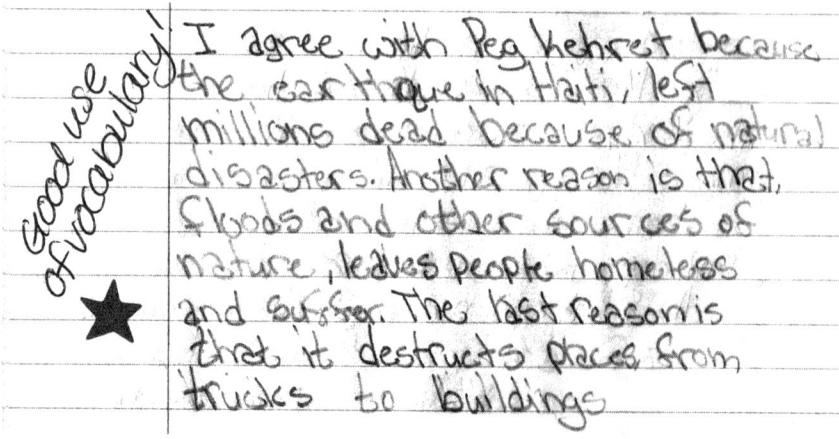

Students receive positive feedback as they practice new vocabulary in their writing.

Naming a Line of Thinking, the Second Check-Stop

As readers pick up new books, they typically establish purposes for reading that carry them through the first few pages or chapters. A reader might select a book to see if it's funny, find out what is happening in the picture on the cover, or determine if a certain prediction about the book will come true. I find that my own book selections are often based on these sorts of criteria. Typically, these purposes are met within the first few chapters, in which all the story elements, including the problem, are generally revealed. This is why book abandonment happens most often during the reading of the first two quadrants of the text. We can end the cyclical process of book abandonment when we ask our students, at the end of the second quadrant, to establish a new purpose for reading.

The purpose of talking and writing to extend thinking is to arrive at one central idea that becomes a theory that readers pursue throughout the rest of the text. I call this theory a *line of thinking*.

When readers name a line of thinking, they establish a new purpose for reading that carries them through the rest of the book. Helping our students form a line of thinking at the end of the second quadrant is critical to building students' interest and stamina in longer texts and avoiding overabandonment. When we help students establish a purpose for reading, we give them an essential tool for comprehension and motivation (Tovani, 2000).

Setting a new purpose for reading by naming a line of thinking is the second check-stop in the C. I. A. approach. At the end of the second quadrant, readers stop to name possible themes and then select the one that is most supported by textual evidence. Usually, lines of thinking become obvious as readers reread entries in their notebooks. Rereading co-created charts, vocabulary lists, and informal writing helps readers recognize patterns and trends in their thinking. Repetition is the author's way of communicating importance, so ideas or words that repeat will point the reader to the theme.

Complex texts may include multiple themes. For the sake of clarity, students should focus on one central theme to pursue throughout the remaining quadrants. Selecting one theme from a list involves determining which idea has the most textual evidence to support it. In addition, knowledge of the genre also impacts the choice of which line of thinking to pursue. Common lines of thinking can be found across genres, and learning to recognize these commonalities will help readers transfer learning into other texts.

Interpreting the Genre

In complex texts, the interactions among characters and ideas in the text will be subtle and deeply embedded (Lewis & Moorman, 2007). Yet readers can rely on the predictable elements of genre to direct them to these subtleties in relationships. Teachers help students simplify the difficult task of identifying inferential patterns in complex text by helping them identify and focus on what is most important. What is most important in the text will be largely influenced by genre. Therefore, knowing the most critical element within a genre helps readers know where to focus their attention while reading.

For example, when reading realistic fiction, the attention of the reader should be drawn to the main character. The main character, in realistic fiction, is the element that has the most influence on the plot. Readers rely on this character evolving over the course of the book in response to his or her circumstances.

Knowing that the main character will be important helps readers narrow their thinking and arrive at possible themes. As an example, in the book *Shiloh* (Naylor, 1991), readers will need to narrow their focus to the main character. Focusing on Marty allows readers to deepen their understanding of his motivations throughout the story. In the book, Marty befriends a dog that is being abused by his owner. Marty's moral code, which calls for him to protect animals, outweighs his desire to do what is right in the eyes of the law. In the second quadrant, readers see how Marty's motivations to save the dog drive the entire plot. This points the reader to the theme of the book, which is that sticking up for what we believe is right often has consequences.

When reading realistic fiction, readers can expect tension to arise as the main character achieves an internal change, often in conjunction with overcoming challenges and/or deciphering right and wrong. The thematic pattern of achieving an awareness of self is predictable and reliable across realistic fiction. Focusing on the most important element, rather than stopping to notice every detail, helps readers draw out what is most critical to the text and also allows them to quicken their reading pace.

Eventually, readers will reach the check-stop at the end of the second quadrant, which requires them to select a theme, or message, that is well supported by the text and genre. Knowing thematic patterns across texts within a genre helps to simplify this task.

Realistic Fiction

Most important element	Character
Readers will think about:	How the main character changes over time. How the main character overcomes challenges. The main character's beliefs about right and wrong. How the main character's circumstances impact his/her choices.

Fantasy

Most important element	Character
Readers will think about:	How the main character changes over time (unexpected hero). How the main character overcomes challenges. How the main character proves goodness. Right vs. wrong, good vs. evil.

Narrative Nonfiction

Most important element	Setting
Readers will think about:	Cause and effect. How circumstances shape one's life. The impact of events on our world. Right vs. wrong.

Nudging Students Toward a Theme

Initially, students will need support as they recognize possible lines of thinking in their notes. Teachers support students through modeling in read-aloud, as well as in individual conferences with them. When modeling, name the thinking students are already doing and nudge them toward something larger.

Upon reaching the end of the second quadrant in the book *The Castle in the Attic* (Winthrop, 1985), I name what students are already thinking by pointing out their entries.

Teacher: Let's look at the entries in our notebooks, looking for patterns in our thinking. Open up to your character chart. Notice how we separated good and bad characters here. This shows me that you have already begun to think about good and evil. This is a theme that is recurring throughout epic fantasy books. Let's add "good versus evil" to our possible lines of thinking. What else do you notice in our entries?

Student 1: We wrote about the Code of Chivalry.

Teacher: And what is the Code of Chivalry?

Student 1: Rules you have to follow in order to be a knight.

Teacher: Who are the knights in this book?

Student 2: Sir Simon, and I think William will be a knight too because it said, "The squire shall cross the drawbridge and the time will be right for a quest" (Winthrop, 1985, p. 80).

Teacher: So you are thinking about how the main character will change throughout the book. You think he will become a knight by following the Code of Chivalry. Could that be a line of thinking?

By naming the thinking students have already done and nudging them toward a larger idea, teachers help students narrow their focus to one important theme. A single line of thinking is selected by considering which theme has the most text evidence to support it and which theme is transferable into other texts of that same genre.

Using the Evidence Collection Box

Once a line of thinking has been named, students will write it down at the top of one of the most important entries in their reader's notebooks: the evidence collection box. The evidence collection box will be the place where students gather evidence to support their line of thinking as they read the third quadrant of the text.

Collect Evidence

Line of thinking: _____

_____

_____

Evidence Collection Box

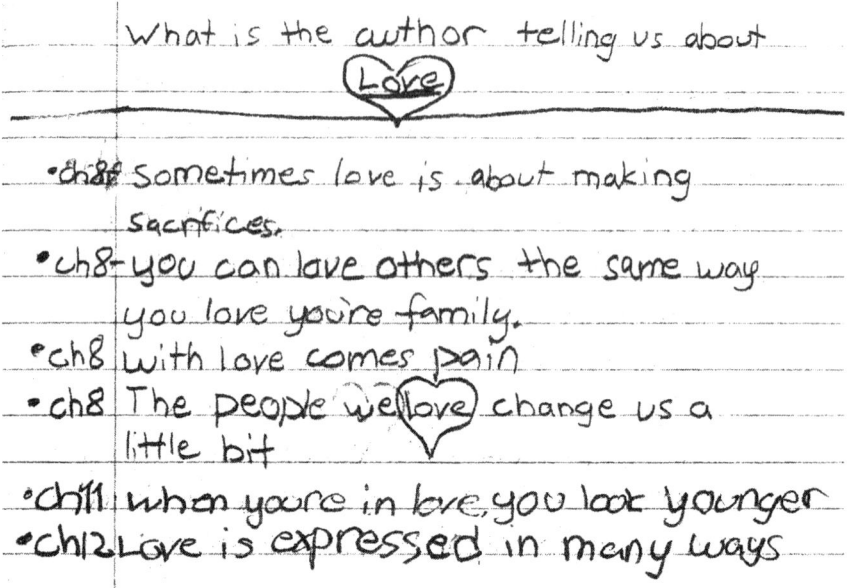

Evidence collection box for Baby *(MacLachlan, 1993).*

I love the above sample of students' thinking about the book *Baby*, by Patricia MacLachlan (1993). Here, the line of thinking is that the author is trying to teach the reader something about love. Naming this theme facilitates deep thought in students, as it leads them to try to make sense of the concept of love through the author's perspective.

This gives us an example of how understanding the theme of a text involves going beyond the literal meaning in order to formulate larger ideas (Fountas & Pinnell, 2006). This movement from literal thinking to inferential thinking is the primary difference between the focuses of the first and second quadrants. Only when students take comprehension up a level on Bloom's Taxonomy (Bloom, 1956) and engage in the work of inferential thinking can they truly interpret the meaning of the text.

Interpreting the Text in Quadrant 3:
Adding Evidence to Support a Line of Thinking

I have never enjoyed putting together puzzles the way my mother does. For me, it takes too much time to get to the good part, the part where the picture becomes more obvious. I simply don't have the patience to labor over the initial tasks of laying the frame, sorting the pieces, and connecting the early patterns. It takes great stamina to get through the initial challenge of puzzle building. If reading is like putting together a puzzle, then I must teach readers that despite the struggles we face early in a text, building our stamina will propel us forward to the good part.

The readers in my classroom who struggle most are not those who score the lowest on assessments, but those who cannot seem to build enough stamina to read longer texts. The C. I. A. approach is designed to support readers through the early quadrants, during which endurance is needed most, and release students to enjoy the remaining quadrants.

Once readers get to the good part, speed quickens. The book becomes easier as the author's message becomes more transparent. No longer is the reader working to figure it out. Rather, the reader works to see the whole picture. What propels the reader at this point in the text is the desire to see all the pieces fall into place, and the closer readers are to the end of the book, the more obvious the picture becomes.

Collecting Evidence to Support a Line of Thinking

As readers press through quadrant two into quadrant three, their sole purpose is to uncover evidence that supports their line of thinking. Not only is this detective work essential for supporting their theory, it also lays the groundwork for longer writing in response to reading.

Readers collect evidence in the evidence collection box, using paraphrases and direct quotes pulled from the text. The way readers paraphrase should clearly demonstrate the link between the event and the theme, as in this example of evidence collected from *Earthquake Terror* (Kehret, 1996):

Line of Thinking: Nature is more powerful than man.

- Nature is so powerful that Jonathan and Abby had to duck and cover (p. 23).
- Nature is so powerful that the camper was destroyed, as well as everything in it (p. 42).
- Man builds a strong bridge, but nature destroys it (p. 52).
- Floodwaters cover the island, showing nature is in control.
- Power lines are knocked down causing fires that destroy buildings (p. 83).
- "Phone's out. Power's out. Water mains are broken" (p. 88).

Collecting evidence to support a line of thinking is the work demanded of students in today's testing era, in which every short-answer response must be supported with evidence from the text. This work also prepares students to critically respond to text, as they become used to questioning its content and reliability—a skill that is certainly timely given the unreliable media sources our students will be exposed to.

While collecting evidence to support a line of thinking, readers might need to stop and revise their line of thinking in response to new evidence. The most likely place for this revision work is at the turning point—the place where the plot makes a dramatic change and the author reveals his or her message. The turning point will be the last piece of evidence added to the evidence collection box.

Identifying the Turning Point

The school district I work in has adopted the Developmental Reading Assessment (Beaver & Carter, 2005) as one of our core assessments of literacy. It tests fluency, accuracy, and comprehension, and we give this assessment to our students three times a year. One of the questions on this assessment asks students to "tell what the most important event was in the story, and give reasons to support your answer." Students typically struggle with this question. I might have six or eight different students taking the same assessment, and all of them will answer this question uniquely. Just as they struggle to answer the question, I struggle to grade it. What *is* the most important event in the story? Is it the student's favorite part, or is there one *best* answer?

The answer to this question has fundamentally changed the way I read and teach reading. Yes, there is one *best* answer to the question found on so many of our district and state tests. The most important event in the story is the event that *changes* the story—the turning point. Referred to in most literature courses as the climax of the book, it is the moment in the story when the plot changes dramatically and the author reveals the message to the reader. Not necessarily the most exciting part, but the place where the ending becomes obvious, the turning point marks the most critical moment in the entire book.

Readers can expect the turning point to appear at the end of the third quadrant, almost without fail. Usually it pops right out at us as we read. Other times, readers may have to stop and reread here in order to understand why a certain event represents the turning point.

When reading *Earthquake Terror* (Kehret, 1996) with my students, I was amazed to find the turning point revealed in the last sentence of the third quadrant. At this point in our read-aloud, we were collecting evidence to show that nature is more powerful than man. Strong text evidence supported this line of thinking. And then, on page 101, we came to the moment when the hero of the book, Jonathan, was overcome by nature. Swimming toward shore through the floodwaters, "Jonathan's feet quit kicking. His arms dangled limply downward. He floated briefly, face down, then sank" (Kehret, 1996). We added this final piece of evidence to our collection box, feeling sure of the author's message.

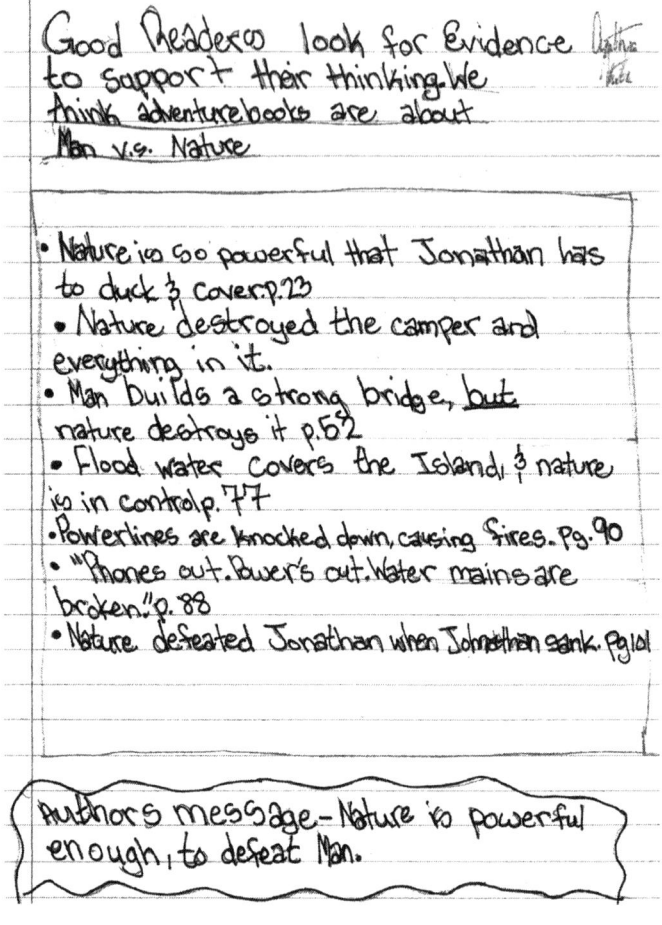

An evidence collection box, with the final piece of evidence being the turning point—the event that reveals the author's message.

Without knowing to look for the turning point at the end of the third quadrant, readers might miss it and, in doing so, misconceive the author's message. In the book *Earthquake Terror* (Kehret, 1996), Jonathan doesn't die. He is pulled out of the water by his loyal dog, Moose, and rescued by a helicopter. Many of my students would consider this to be the most exciting part in the text—the climax of the story. Basing their interpretation of the author's message on this dramatic moment would certainly alter their perception of what Peg Kehret tells us in this book. If our students are going to do well on high-stakes tests, they must get this right!

To communicate the significance of the turning point, all thinking in the third quadrant of the text should be focused on predicting and identifying it. In quadrant three, the author typically uses foreshadowing to prepare us for the turning point. Readers slow down to notice this crafting and to consider what the author wants the reader to predict.

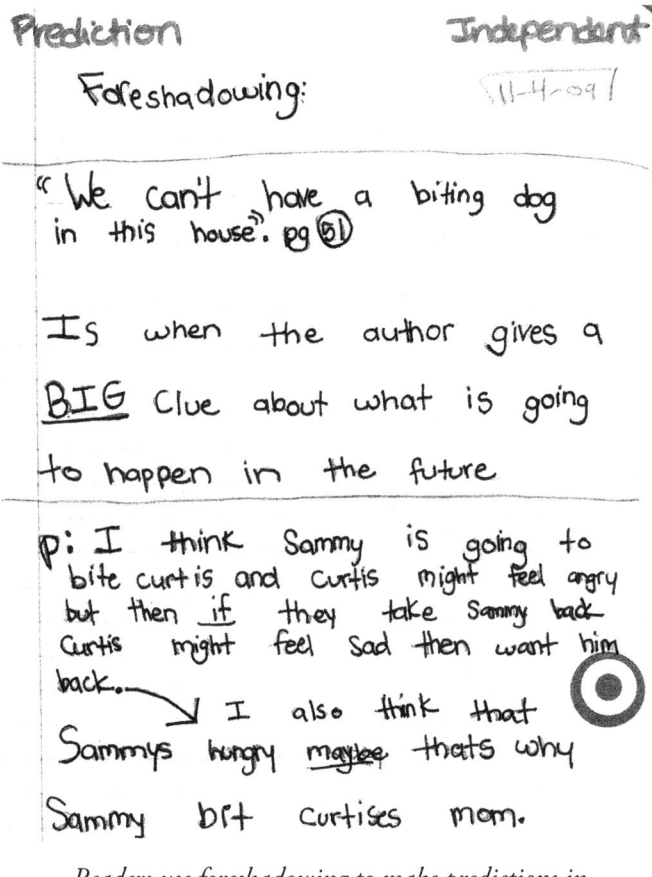

Readers use foreshadowing to make predictions in
One Small Dog *(Hurwitz, 2002).*

Constantly reminding students of what the turning point is and of its importance will ensure that students recognize it when they see it. I like to have students mark the end of the third quadrant with a bright pink sticky note, so that they are reminded to stop and reflect at that point. This reflection will be the third check-stop in the C. I. A. model.

Reflecting on the Turning Point, the Third Check-Stop

Calkins writes that nearing the end of a book is like reaching the top of a mountain. You linger there and look back at the whole view (2001). The panorama is beautiful and, yes, this beauty is the reason for the journey. You feel a sense of accomplishment in this moment, though the work is not yet over. An entire trail lies below, leading back down the mountain.

To me, the top of the mountain is not the *end* of the book but the turning point—the place where the author reveals his or her message. At the turning point, readers stop to look at the culmination of the story, considering everything that led to that point. Here, readers see the text from a new perspective: that of the author. The view is breathtaking as you take in the overall composition of the journey.

Upon reaching the turning point, students will learn to stop and reflect on this critical event. In their notebooks, students describe the event in the book that they believe is the turning point, and they support their thinking by describing how this event will change the story. Students go on to describe how this one event communicates the author's message. Finally, they make a prediction as to how the story will end.

Turning Point Writing

I think the turning point of the book is…
This will change the plot because…
I think this event tells me that the author's message is…
I predict…

The book *Children of the Dust Bowl* (Stanley, 1992) tells the story of one million Oklahoma families that lost everything they owned during the Great Depression and the Dust Bowl. They were forced to make a treacherous journey across the desert landscape, facing unthinkable hardships along the way. When they arrived in California, desperately seeking employment, they were met with prejudice and injustice. Even as the government sought to improve their living conditions, Okies were being treated as unwelcome outsiders and tormented because of their visible poverty. Young children suffered dearly, believing their lives to be hopeless. One man with great courage—Leo Hart—stood up for the rights of those suffering children. At the three-quarter mark, Stanley reveals Leo Hart's resolute belief that Okie children should be given the same rights as others. At this turning point, students stop to expose the author's message.

Good Readers look for
the turning point and
make a prediction and think
about the authors message

(Turning Point)
T.P: Leo Hart decides to build a
school for the Okie children
that would help them get
the same opportunities as
others

A.M: No matter who you are
everyone deserves the
same opportunities to fulfill
their hopes and dreams.

Prediction: I predict that the
Okie children will have more
opportunities and reach their
hopes and dreams because
of the new school.

Turning point writing for Children of the Dust Bowl
(Stanley, 1992).

Assessing at the Turning Point

To meet rigorous standards and succeed on high-stakes tests, our students must be able to identify the most important event in a story, and the author's message. Therefore, one of the most critical places to stop and assess students is here at the turning point.

I like to draw close to students in one-on-one conferences at this critical check-point. In these friendly conversations, I am able to identify the thought processes of my students and determine their greatest needs. In most cases, I am pleasantly surprised at their abilities. This was the case when I conferenced with Maggie, a below-level reader who, for most of the school year, had struggled to read independently.

Maggie had been reading the book *The Battle for the Castle* (Winthrop, 1994) in her independent reading. She had selected it after our class had finished reading its prequel, *The Castle in the Attic* (Winthrop, 1985), in read-aloud. I worried that the book would be too difficult for her but was surprised by her interest and stamina. As she arrived at the turning point, I met with her in a conference.

Teacher: So, I haven't read the ending to *The Battle for the Castle* yet, so you are going to be teaching me something today about the turning point in this book. Tell me about the turning point.

Maggie: I think the turning point is when William never gives up on the people that are depending on him to defeat the rats because they already know he is the hero because he was the one who defeated Alastor. This will change the story because soon Jason will realize that William was brave and that is what William wanted to show Jason. They author's message is that you can never give up just like William never gave up on defeating the rats.

Teacher: Interesting…so what you are saying is that William didn't have to prove that he was a hero because he had already proven that he was a hero in the first book. So now he has to prove that he is *still* a hero. Is that what he had to do?

Maggie: Yeah.

Teacher: So, even now, in this new situation, he can still be heroic like he was in the first story. Was there a specific event when you knew that he was going to defeat the rats?

Maggie: Um, well, I think it was the part where a rat bit him… and…um…his leg was hurt but he was still fighting. He still was like checking if everything was okay. They were like in a dungeon and it was dark and he didn't like dark spaces with no windows and stuff. But he was determined and never gave up even though he was hurt and he got better.

Teacher: Can you think of a word that describes "never give up"?

Maggie: Um…determined?

Teacher: Any others that we have learned this year that mean "never give up"?

Maggie: Um…brave?

Teacher: Uh-huh…Brave has something to do with "never give up." So we read *Earthquake Terror* (Kehret, 1996), when Jonathan showed he was brave. We read *Poppy* (Avi, 1995), where Poppy showed she was brave. And we read *The Castle in the Attic* (Winthrop, 1985), where William showed he was brave. In all those books, what have you learned about bravery? What does bravery mean to you?

Maggie: When you, like you're going through hard stuff and you like try to save somebody or protect somebody you need to be brave to go through all the tests. And you have to um…never give up.

Teacher: Even if you're feeling…

Maggie: Afraid.

Teacher: Yeah, good thinking. So, do you think this will help you in your own life?

Maggie: Yes.

Teacher: When might you remember these books? Can you think of a time when it might help you?

Maggie: Um…probably when I am going through hard stuff, like college.

Teacher: Oh, good! You've got plans to go to college!

Every time I read through these conference notes, I tear up because I know Maggie's story and am inspired by her last words. Maggie, like so many other students in my classroom, did not begin the year with hopes of college. Many students have already pegged themselves into other categories, not recognizing their full potential. Raising the expectations of our students, and supporting them as they work toward successfully meeting high educational standards, breaks the barriers they have placed on themselves. Aligning classroom instruction to the Common Core State Standards has the power to change the courses of our students' lives (CCSSI, 2010). If we prepare every student for the demands of college, every one of them will begin to see college as a real possibility.

Applying the Text
to Other Areas of Life,
in Quadrant 4:
Evaluating the Author's Message

When I think about my life as a reader, certain books stand out as landmarks—books that I will continue to recall long after reading them because their contents somehow changed or affected the way I think about the world. I believe that the act of reading has the potential to shape who we are as people. Books help us define and reflect on our beliefs.

Good readers know to read with the expectation that every book will have some impact on their lives. They read with the purpose of discovering the author's message, and they use that message to weigh their own beliefs. This type of thinking takes practice. Readers must be trained and coached toward this thinking. This coaching is best done in the context of rich, complex literature.

When we expose readers to rich, complex, sophisticated texts, we give them the opportunity to learn how books can change their lives. This is why it is so important for teachers to thoughtfully select books for students to read. While there is value in giving students choice in what they read, our desire is that they make *wise* book choices. Therefore, we must expose them to books we know they will love, even though they wouldn't necessarily pick those books themselves.

I relate limiting reading choices to the way we train our children to eat a variety of foods. If I were to give my five-year-old daughter the opportunity to select her own dinner meal, I know that, night after night, her choice would be chicken nuggets. By allowing her to make her own dinner choices, I clearly would be restricting her ability to meet her nutritional needs. At the same time, she would never learn to love other, delicious foods.

I think all parents recognize the benefits of broadening their children's interest in food by requiring them to try new things, but doing so requires diligent effort on the parents' part. In the same way, we must remain diligent in broadening our students' reading interests by requiring them to try new genres and authors. With this more controlled approach, we ensure that the books students read will be landmark books: "books that remain in someone's mind long after the last page is read" (Angelillo, 2003, p. 33).

While reading *Children of the Dust Bowl* (Stanley, 1992) in readaloud, I selected the book *Out of the Dust* (Hesse, 1999) as a book club book. I knew that all students in my class would be able to access this text in guided practice, due to the extensive background knowledge they had built through our reading of *Children of the Dust Bowl*. Yet, even as I introduced the book to my class, I had second thoughts about my book selection. I worried that the boys in my classroom would not be inspired by the girl character, the prose structure, and the genre—historical fiction. I knew that the book was one they would never choose to read on their own. Despite my doubts, my instincts told me to follow through with this selection. In the end, several of my boys chose it as their favorite book of the school year.

Seeing the Whole Picture

At the end of quadrant three, when readers reach the turning point, it is like seeing the whole picture in the puzzle before all the pieces are in place. You know what the puzzle is going to look like in the end, but you don't feel a full sense of accomplishment yet. You must quickly place the final pieces. Laying the final pieces of the puzzle is the easy work of the last quadrant.

Thinking back to my mother's puzzle-a-thons, I remember the extravagance that went into placing the final piece. Rather than quietly snapping the piece in, my mother would complete her work with a loud "ta-da!" Everyone in the house knew that she had finished her puzzle. Throughout the following week we were reminded of her accomplishment, as the puzzle was left on the table for all to appreciate. Every so often, I would spot my mother stopping to admire her puzzle before walking by it. She was proud of her accomplishment, and her glance down at the puzzle reminded her of the difficult, persistent work that it represented.

Good readers relish a book long after its completion. They reflect on their thinking and consider how the message of the book might apply to their lives.

Reading to the End

As I get close to finishing a good book, I always make sure I have an uninterrupted block of time in which I can read to the end. I want readers to know the importance of this in their own reading lives. I want them to understand how one's reading pace gradually picks up speed, with momentum being strongest near the end.

It is during the last quadrant of our read-aloud book that I schedule an uninterrupted block of reading time, to allow students to feel this momentum. Sometimes I am able to get through the entire last quadrant in one sitting. In longer text, I break the last quadrant up and read it over two days. In any case, students feel as though we have closed a door to the outside world so that we can linger in the enjoyment of reading.

Processing Thinking in the Last Quadrant

Processing thinking in the last quadrant of the text is different from the work done in the first three quadrants. No longer are readers reading to "figure it out." At this stage, readers are simply confirming the thinking they have already done. In this quadrant of the text, the reader's notebook will simply serve as a reference tool. No longer will it be necessary for students to stop and write thinking down or chart information. Stopping points during the last quadrant are sporadic and brief—their purpose here is to allow students the opportunity to talk at the times when it will be difficult for them to remain quiet. Rather than focusing conversations around a turn and talk stem, teachers will allow for open-ended thought. Simply saying "turn and talk" will give students an opportunity to engage in quick dialogue. This dialogue will synthesize and extend their thinking about the text.

Completing a Formal Reflection, the Final Check-Stop

Last night, my daughter selected the book *Seven Blind Mice* (Young, 1992) as her bedtime story. I couldn't help but realize that this book provides a beautiful illustration of what it means to synthesize learning. In the story, the seven blind mice find "a strange something." Each day, one of them investigates the something and, on returning to the others, describes what he or she felt. "It's a pillar," says the first mouse, after touching the something's leg. "It's a snake," says the second mouse, after touching the something's trunk. The last mouse to investigate the something runs across it from end to end. This mouse thinks about all the other descriptions, putting them together with his own thinking. In his wisdom, the mouse learns that the something is, in fact, an elephant. Young concludes with this mouse moral: "Knowing in part may make a fine tale, but wisdom comes in seeing the whole" (Young, 1992, p. 32).

Before applying the text to their lives, readers must "see the whole"; they must synthesize their learning. The process of synthesizing after reading is multifaceted, as readers first summarize the text, then generalize the author's message, and then evaluate that message in light of other information. Therefore, the final check-stop for readers in the C. I. A. model is stopping to write a formal reflection that incorporates these tasks.

Formal Reflection Frame

Paragraph 1: Synthesis Summary	
Introduction Sentence	*The book _____, by _____, tells about _____.*
Body	Tell the events of the book in 5–7 sentences.
Concluding Sentence	*In conclusion, _____ _____.*
Paragraph 2: Author's Message	
Introduction Sentence	*I think the author's message is _____.*
Body	State the evidence from the book that supports this thinking.
Concluding Sentence	*It is clear, _____ _____.*
Paragraph 3: Evaluate the Author's Message	
Introduction Sentence	*I agree/disagree with the author's message.* *I think _____ _____.*
Body	State evidence from outside sources or your own life that supports your thinking.
Concluding Sentence	*As you can see, _____ _____.*

After reading *Earthquake Terror* (Kehret, 1996), students summarize the story and come to a conclusion about the author's message. The detailed work of collecting evidence to support a line of thinking that they have already done offers a range of evidence to support their thinking during this final stage. Students easily evaluate the message that nature is more powerful than man and consider world events that show nature's powerful force. In the end, students organize their own opinions around evidence collected from the text and their own lives.

End of the book Summary

The book, Earthquake Terror by Peg Kehret tells how the Palmers survive a disastrous earthquake. First, Jonathan and Abby are left on Magpie Island after Mrs. Palmer breaks her ankle. Next, a massive earthquake damages Northern California, leaving Jonathan and Abby stranded on the island, dependent on rescuers to save them. As if that isn't bad enough the earthquake causes a flood to destroy the entire island. Jonathan and Abby have to work together to survive, and in the end, they're rescued. Peg Kehret makes it clear, nature is powerful enough to defeat man.

<u>Authors Message</u>

In this book, Peg Kehret wants us to know that nature is strong enough to destroy man. In this book, nature destroys a bridge built by man as if eating a piece of cake. The forces of nature causes a huge camper being destroyed by a gigantic redwood. Clearly you can see that nature is very powerful that it can destroy man but if it couldn't get any worse nature defeats ← Evaluation Jonathan himself. I agree with Peg Kehret because of the earthquake in Haiti. Forces of Nature destroyed ~~tow~~ houses, building, and even injured andkilled many People. I also read about a earthquake in Northern California. The earthquake caused 63 deaths and injurned 3,757 People. Just because of Forces of Nature it cost 11 billion dollars to repair things. Clearly, Nature is able to defeat man.

One student's formal reflection for the book Earthquake Terror *(Kehret, 1996).*

While the writing work of reflecting is lengthy, students look forward to this step in the process as it allows them the opportunity to form their own opinions based on the evidence they have so diligently gathered. The final step in reflection, evaluating the author's message, communicates to students that they have the right to their own thinking. Here students are empowered to take a critical stance—a posture that students must carry as they navigate the unfiltered world of mass media.

Responding to the Author's Message

"The worth of a book is to be measured by what you can carry away from it" (Bernard, 1988). Whether you agree or disagree with the author's message, each book that we read impacts the way we think and respond to the world around us. It is not only our pleasure, but also our responsibility to consider how an author's message applies to our lives, and react to that message accordingly.

When students read *Children of the Dust Bowl* (Stanley, 1992), they must acknowledge the responsibility of ensuring that the message of the book is carried forward. The message that all children deserve the same opportunities to fulfill their hopes and dreams is one that the author wants readers to act on.

Likewise, when students read *Shiloh* (Naylor, 1991), they will form their own beliefs about animal rights and determine for themselves the best way to act on those beliefs. Not every student will pick up a picket sign or pull out a pen and paper, but as teachers we must ensure that our students know that it is within their power to do so. We all have powerful voices that can be used to make a difference in our world. This is what I want my students to know.

I will never forget the experience of watching the movie *City of Ember* (Kenan, 2009) with my students after we had finished reading the book on which it was based in read-aloud. My students had begged me to let them watch the movie, and I agreed, after first warning them that they would be extremely disappointed with the media version of the story. (This warning may have made them even more excited to see it.)

As my students began to watch, there was a subtle hum of talking in the room. Listening in on their conversations, I could tell that students were shocked at the director's interpretation. By the time we reached the part where Doon was being attacked by a giant-size bug, students were livid. "This isn't science fiction, this is fantasy!" one shouted. At the movie's finale, several students asked if we could write a letter to the director.

As the teacher in this situation, I could hardly disguise the smile on my face. I was pleased to know that the students in my classroom had learned that they have a right to their own opinions and perspectives. Most astounding, they knew that their opinions were important and could be powerfully expressed through writing.

> Dear Gil kenan, I read the book
> City of Ember with my class. we begged
> our teacher to watch. the movie we
> all regreted that.
> One thing I liked about the book was
> it had a metiphor for the city; it was a sighn
> of the symbol of life, tyranny and expressed a
> dire cercomstance. That also made the book so
> much more suspenceful
> I liked having the book suspenceful
> did you? Probrobly not because the movie
> wasn't. I thought the escap path was down at
> the edge of the river in the boat room. Not behind
> the wierd lockers.
> Oh! One more thing the book was you changed
> the genre from science fiction to fantacy. And dont
> even get me started on the characters
> I could have picked better with my eyes closed
> wile spining and eating fudge.
> All right I am sick of righting to you
> please try a little harder next time or youre
> gonna have to deal with my friends thunder
> and lightning.
>
>   Youre City of Ember Move disliker
>   Brock
>
>   P.S. Please wright back. Cough Not

In this letter to the director of the movie City of Ember, *Gil Kenan (2009), the writer's voice is clearly expressed through the use of sarcasm.*

Sharing Thinking in Formal Writing—The Optional *S*

When given a *real* audience with which to share their thinking, students become motivated to write about their reading. "All we need is a good reason of our own to write something, and an audience of at least one person we can give it to when it is finished" (Wood Ray, 2002, p. 9). When readers write about their thinking in connection with text, they process information and ideas while simultaneously communicating those ideas to others. There are many authentic forms of writing about reading in the world. You can find genres of writing about reading in literary magazines, newspapers, blogs, and online book clubs. The existence of numerous examples within these genres proves that expert readers write; they write in response to the desire to expand their thinking, share their opinions, and become part of a literature community.

Some examples of authentic genres of writing about reading include letters, book reviews, and literary essays. I encourage you to use these genres to promote further writing about reading in your classroom.

Letters

Sharing opinions or thoughts in response to reading is done very naturally through letter writing. Audiences for such letters might include other readers, authors, or editors. When one is writing a letter, the content of the letter is driven by the purpose for writing the letter. Therefore, the content will change according to the audience. Generally, writing letters will give readers the opportunity to share their thinking about what they have read and ask questions of an audience in order to generate a response.

Dear Jeanne Duprau,

My name is Dena ▇▇▇▇▇ and I'm a 5th grader at Discovery Elementary school in Everett WA. I live with my mom dad and 4 year old brother. My favorite activity is to cook, and to read. My class just finished reading your fabulous book The City of Ember. It was great!

I love the way you described that the people of Ember don't even know what most of the words or things that we have in the present! When my teacher, Mrs. Collinge read the book out loud to the class, I visualized the city just like the worm that Doon kept in his box. At the end of the book, I noticed that right when Lina and Doon found the way out of Ember; the worm was in a cocoon and came out as a moth.

I think that the theme of the book is that knowledge is power, because when Lina and Doon figured out what the instructions said they had the power to find the way out of Ember.

How did you think of the idea of writing The City of Ember? Is The City of Ember your first science fiction novel? Do you live in the United States? Do you have kids that are in love with your books?

In conclusion I really loved your wonderful book The City of Ember. By the way, I really liked the movie and thought that it was sad, but what frustrated me the most was that in the book, the bugs were small which made the book science fiction. But in the movie, the bugs were huge! Which made it fantasy. I really hope that you write back! Please do!

Your biggest fan,

Dena ▇▇▇▇▇

Letter to Jeanne DuPrau, author of The City of Ember *(2003).*

Book Reviews

Students love writing book reviews in response to reading because doing so gives them an opportunity to share their opinions about an author's writing style. A book review typically begins with an exciting lead that encourages someone to read the book. A teaser summary then tells important events from the beginning and middle, but never the end, of the book. Finally, the review persuades the audience further, giving them multiple reasons for reading the book. Sometimes a rating or age recommendation is given. Posting book reviews in the classroom or throughout the school encourages a literate community.

Haley

Writing

Book Review: <u>Knights and Castles</u>

<u>By Will Osborne and Mary Pope – Osborne</u>

In the book Knights and Castles is an amazing book about the middle ages and medieval wars. This book would suite readers who love adventures and Castles. Also for those who want to learn about Knights, Kings, Lords and Ladies how they live and do war. They also say how a Page becomes a squire then a knight. At a dubbing ceremony the king announces that the squire becomes an official Knight.

You will notice diagrams, Fun facts, Pictures and more! Especially diagrams of castles and knights. The book tells the story about King Arthur and the round table. At the actual restaurants they have a stone with a sword stuck in it, they say only a true knight can pull it out. The book also talks about inside the castle and how knights fight and how they celebrate to win. I enjoyed this book at all parts, but mostly I love that it made you feel like you were really in the castle.

Knights and Castles are good for ages 8-12 and grades 3rd-7th. If I had to rate this book I would give it 4 stars out of 5 stars because of how much fun filled adventures they have in the book

Student book review of Knights and Castles *(Osborne & Osborne, 2000).*

Literary Essays

The work of naming a line of thinking and supporting a line of thinking with text evidence is easily shared in the form of a literary essay. Literary essays push readers to examine a big idea and to provide ample evidence to support it. Starting in third grade, students can begin to compose the sophisticated writing typical of literary essays. Literary essays often consist of three to five paragraphs, with an introduction, body paragraph(s), and conclusion.

Caleb

2/17/2011

Code of chivalry

On William's quest to get the necklace from the evil wizard Alastor, He used the code of chivalry to overcome many tests. William used compassion, honesty, and forgiveness I can use these same knightly characteristics to overcome tests in my life.

First, William used compassion to do one of code of chivalry. (Someone who is compassionate to helps others who is in need) William climbed a large apple tree to get an apple for an old man who was starving when William is hungry and thirsty. I have shown compassion when my parents told me to go to school when I was really sleepy.

Next, William also did honesty from code of chivalry. (An honest person tells the truth and believes in the truth) William also show honesty when Calandar's grandson and William tells Calander's grandson about Sir Simon even when he kinda don't believed in him. I have shown honesty (Actually I believed in truth) When my brother said that he "went to the bathroom." I know he was lying.

Finally, William third code of chivalry was forgiveness. (Someone who show forgiveness will be kind their enemy) William showed forgiveness when William freed the dragon from the Alastor's curse. I have shown forgiveness when my brother draw on my homework.

In the conclusion of the rules of chivalry helped William beat the evil wizard Alastor and makes it through the forest with illusions. They also helped me going through tough times when I really need it and make me a better person.

Literary essay written in response to the read-aloud of The Castle in the Attic *(Winthrop, 1985).*

Children of the Dust Bowl Essay
By Jonathan
December, 2009

The Okies were people who lived in the panhandle who faced many hardships during the time of 1929 – 1941. The term Okie stands for pride, courage, and determination. The Okies were deserving of this name because they worked hard to overcome hardship and provide for their families.

The Okies showed courage when they migrated from Oklahoma to California on Route 66. First, they had to cross mountain ranges that were very steep. The Okies took their jalopies up roads without guardrails and often "walked to the summit rather than drive an unreliable car." After that, the Okies had to cross the Mojave Desert in the conditions of 120 degrees. Radiators cracked, tires popped, and cars broke down. But the Okies never gave up hope and they kept going. The Okies showed great courage by continuing to travel even though it was difficult.

The Okies were determined to reach California and get a job in order to have money to feed their families. The Okies were so determined to get to California that they sold all their belongings just to get to California. After getting a car they packed all their possessions and six or more kids in the car. Then, they kept going on the mother road even though it was very risky. When they finally got to California they realized that they were lied to about California. The Okies were determined to get a job even though there were few jobs in California. The jobs they had only payed them the wage of 25 – 30 cents an hour.

The Okies were people who felt proud of themselves because they didn't give up despite many hardships. Farming in Oklahoma wasn't easy and the Okies had to work hard. There were times when there was little or no rain. Some farmers had to sell machinery to get money. Some farmers had to borrow money from the bank to pay bills because their crops were failing. Soon farmers houses were pushed down by a tractor because they could not pay the landlord. After that, a big storm came and soon the Okies could no longer farm because it was impossible, but they were able to survive.

In conclusion, the Okies were deserving of their name that means, pride, courage and determination.

Literary essay written in response to the book Children of the Dust Bowl *(Stanley, 1992).*

Mentor Text

Teaching students the genres of writing about reading begins with studying real-world examples. Part of this study involves analyzing these genres to determine their critical elements. When selecting mentor text, teachers should search for writing that is at a slightly higher level than the level of writing expected of their students. Choosing sophisticated samples gives students a feeling that their writing has the potential to be *this* good (Wood Ray, 2006). Mentor text can be drawn from real-world samples or past student work. While reading these mentor texts with students, teachers model the highlighting and marking of elements of the genre, noting what belongs in this type of writing and how the writing is organized. From this study, teachers and students can work together to create frames and rubrics for each genre.

The Writing Process

The idea of formal writing is that students complete all steps outlined in the writing process and thereby produce a polished, published piece. The stages of the writing process are:

- Planning
- Drafting
- Revising
- Editing
- Publishing
- Sharing

Much of the planning work will have already been done in student notebook entries. Before writing, students look back over their collections to consider what might belong in the genre they have selected.

For example, when writing a book review, students will include a teaser summary of the book, which reveals important story elements without giving away the book's ending. Students who are writing book reviews will be able to use the summaries they have already written to plan for this type of writing.

During the drafting stage of formal writing, students get their thinking written down on paper outside of their reader's notebooks. Although drafts will be revised and edited, students should strive to do their best work in the drafting stage, to make revision and editing simpler and less overwhelming.

As students prepare to formally publish their writing, consider authentic ways of sharing their writing. If the students write letters, make sure that those letters are delivered. Most authors post an address or e-mail for sending fan letters. Book reviews can be published online, in literary magazines, or on school websites. Essays can become part of a classroom collection, or can be sent to literary magazines and contests.

It is my experience that when students are given an authentic context for sharing their writing, they are more apt to produce polished work.

Assessing Formal Writing

Assessing formal writing is about defining quality. By using thoughtfully chosen mentor text, teachers set a target for the quality of writing expected of students. Together, teacher and students can create rubrics that define expectations for each genre of formal writing. Involving students in the creation of rubrics "helps them [the students] internalize the criteria and bring them to bear on their own work" (Stiggins et al., 2006, p. 209). In this process, we move from using rubrics to simply provide a score to using them to teach students to recognize the elements of quality writing. If rubrics are well crafted, with student involvement, then students will be successful in evaluating their own writing using these rubrics. The more teachers include students in the assessment process, the better understanding students will have of quality writing.

Writing Across Content Areas

Probably the most constant complaint I hear from teachers is that there is not enough quality instruction time available during the school day. It is true; teachers are bombarded with interruptions that often take away instructional time. Without nullifying this complaint, I do believe teachers can reclaim instructional time by prioritizing instruction across the school day. One way to do this is by making writing a priority in all content areas. In doing so, teachers will increase the amount of necessary practice students receive in writing.

Requiring a formal writing piece from each of my students at the end of each chapter book read-aloud unit ensures that every student will write five *formal* papers in the fifth-grade year, not to mention the amount of *informal* writing they will have penned in their reader's notebooks. Broadening written work across math, science, and social studies guarantees that students will complete another six or more *formal* writing pieces within the year. Simply by infusing the essential elements of literacy across the school day, we can reprioritize our time.

Visualizing the Year

My family used to take road trips during the summer to places like Disneyland, Glacier National Park, and Teton Village. Despite the long hours in the car, these road trips, each with its own unexpected adventures and slight detours along the way, became favorite childhood memories.

One unforgettable road trip stands out in my memories. My family and I were on our way to Yellowstone National Park for a family reunion. After a long day of driving in order to "make good time," we pulled into a small Montana town. This was the only night we had not made overnight reservations for.

There were only two places to stay—rustic-looking cabins or the Motel 6. My dad, of course, voted for the Motel 6. My sister and I begged to stay in the cabins. In an effort to give us the vacation of our dreams, Dad eventually gave in.

This unplanned adventure would be one we would laugh about for years. I remember placing my flip-flops right next to the bed, refusing to walk on the dirty shag carpet. Scared of spiders, I slept on top of the covers. This night in the cabins turned out to be the most remembered event of our vacation, probably because of its spontaneity.

Teaching is very much like the well-planned family road trip. Despite careful planning, there are always necessary pit stops and unexpected detours. Being prepared for the dynamics of responsive instruction allows teachers to plan tomorrow's mini-lessons in response to what students are doing today (Fletcher & Portalupi, 2001).

Reaching June Goals Using the Gradual Release Model

Despite a spontaneous overnight stay, our family made it to our ultimate destination on time, mostly due to my father's tedious trip planning and my mother's skills at reading a road map. In classrooms, teachers "road-map" the year by considering the end goals first. They ask, "What do my students need to know and be able to do when they leave my classroom in June?" These end goals are defined by standards outlined for the grade level. Once June goals are set, teachers consider the halfway target: "If students must be here in June, how far do they need to be toward accomplishing this goal in January?"

By the time my fifth-graders leave my classroom, I want them to be confident readers who understand what good readers do and who count themselves among them. I want students to have a wide interest in books, due to common experiences with meaningful texts. I want them to be active participants in a literate community, in which oral and written response is a purposeful reading habit.

These are large goals, but they are accomplishable if supportive classroom routines—classroom routines that carry readers through the gradual release of responsibility—are in place.

The gradual release model, first developed by Pearson and Gallagher (1983), outlines stages of explicit instruction that guide readers from modeling to guided practice and independence. When planning the instructional scope and sequence for the year, it is important to focus the planning around this model, always allowing ample time for modeling and guided practice before expecting students to work independently.

Modeling in Read-Aloud: The First Layer of Planning

Our work as teachers always begins with explicit modeling. Therefore, when planning your literacy scope and sequence, teacher modeling in read-aloud is the first structure you will want to lay out over a year.

My June goals define the read-aloud block, which I use to expose my students to a variety of genres so that these genres become as comfortable to them as a series book would be. After considering what genres I want to expose students to, I lay those genres out over the year.

Long Term Planning for the Reading Workshop: First Layer

	Sept.	Oct.	Nov.	Dec.	Jan.	Feb.	March	April	May	June
Read Aloud	Realistic Fiction		Realistic Fiction		Historical Fiction		Nonfiction		Science Fiction	

Read-aloud genres selected for fifth grade and placed on the calendar at the beginning of the school year.

Guided Practice in Small Groups: The Second Layer of Planning

While providing grade-level instruction for all students within the structure of a read-aloud is critical, it will not allow students the opportunity to practice strategies in their own readable texts, at their own instructional levels. Therefore, we must also provide differentiated instruction in the reading workshop block.

Guided Reading

Early fluent and newly fluent readers will need guidance as they work to first decode and then comprehend text. These readers will need the highest level of support that is provided in guided reading and transitional guided reading. I will not be discussing these structures, due to their focus on early reading skills. To answer your questions about this instructional approach, I recommend seeking out other resources. The book *Guided Reading* would be a credible place to start your research (Fountas & Pinnell, 1996).

Book Clubs

The next level of small-group instruction is appropriate for fluent and proficient readers. I like to use the term "book club" to describe the small-group setting appropriate for these readers. The term simply refers to a group of students reading the same book, who meet together to discuss the book several times throughout the experience.

There are many ways to organize book clubs in your classroom. Some book clubs are organized homogeneously, with students at similar reading levels placed together. Other book clubs are organized heterogeneously, with students placed in groups according to reading interest alone. While some book clubs remain constant throughout the school year, other book clubs disband and regroup throughout the year.

I am not going to tell you which type of book clubs to set up in your classroom. I believe you must pick the type of book club arrangement that works best for you and your students. It may look different from year to year, depending on the students you have. That is the way it should be. Our classrooms should be thoughtfully constructed to support the needs of learners.

Through trial and error, I have learned to abide by a few book club rules that seem to make these groups more manageable. They are:

- Limit groups to 4–6 students.
- Assign each person in the group a partner.
- Use the C. I. A. model to plan book club assignments.
- Train partners to support each other during independent reading.
- Expect students to come to book club meetings with thoughts written down.
- Teach students to use turn and talk stems in book club discussions.
- Meet with book clubs at the end of each quadrant.
- Support book club members through conferences between book club meetings.

Partnerships

Different from paired reading partnerships, in which students read text together, helping each other figure out difficult words, partnerships within book clubs are set up primarily to offer comprehension support. Book club partners are trained to rely on each other to clarify comprehension, support each other in completing assignments, and hold each other accountable for those assignments. Partners do not sit beside each other reading the text together. Instead, they read alone, meeting to talk about the book when necessary.

Before bringing the entire group together for formal discussion at the end of each quadrant, it is helpful to allow time for partners to meet and share their thinking with one another. This gets students "warmed-up" for the work of talking in a larger group. It also adds an accountability piece. Meeting with a partner before the book club meeting often solves the problem of unpreparedness.

Assignments

Book club assignments and meetings can easily be centered on the framework of the C. I. A. approach. The first time a book club meets, students use a blank calendar to set target deadlines for completing the work of each quadrant. This calendar mirrors the timing of each stage of the C. I. A. process. More time is given for reading in the first two quadrants than in the last two quadrants.

While reading quadrant one, students will be responsible for keeping a character list, a setting map or setting clues list, a list of the important events, and a list of the problems described in the book. Students might also use one or two selected turn and talk stems as a writing frame. At the end of quadrant one, students will bring this work to the second book club meeting, in which they share their charts and thinking with the larger group in ways that will help them monitor and organize their thinking. After this meeting, students return to their seats to write a summary of the first quadrant.

While reading quadrant two, students will continue to chart, but will focus their charting around the element that is most critical to the genre. For example, readers might focus on the main character, tracking his or her character traits. In addition, students might be assigned an informal writing piece. At the end of quadrant two, the book club will meet for a third time, to discuss possible themes and determine a line of thinking for the book. In this meeting, group members will add an evidence collection box to their reader's notebooks.

Quadrant three will challenge students to locate text evidence that supports their line of thinking. They will add these pieces of evidence to their evidence collection boxes. In addition, students will be noticing foreshadowing and will be writing their predictions in their notebooks. Students will come to the fourth book meeting to discuss the turning point. Upon finishing this discussion, students will be sent back to their seats to begin working on their turning point writing.

In the final quadrant of the book club book, students will generally not be responsible for assignments. Instead, they will be given more liberty to sit back and enjoy the book. A final book club meeting will allow students the opportunity to discuss the ending and evaluate the author's message. Students will then write a formal reflection that conveys their understanding of the book.

Meeting with Students

I used to break my back trying to meet with every book club every week. As I repeatedly failed in this attempt, I began to have feelings of inadequacy about my teaching and management abilities. After months of being distraught, I finally sat back to reanalyze. Teaching shouldn't be this hard; there must be a better way. Why was I feeling the need to meet with every group every week? Was doing so really necessary?

By trying to meet with every book club group every week, I was setting myself up for failure. I was also limiting the time students spent actually reading. The C. I. A. approach has freed me to meet with book clubs when it is most critical, at the end of each quadrant. In between these large book club meetings, I draw in close to examine the work students are doing in their partnerships. This routine is manageable for me, and allows me to meet with students when they need me most.

During book club meetings I remain mostly an observer and coach. Just as when I'm listening in on turn and talk, I sit back and let students lead the conversation. They know to use the turn and talk framework of sharing and responding to guide the book club discussion. Students are trained to respond to someone else's thinking first, before sharing their own. They are also trained to ensure that everyone in the group gets the opportunity to speak. I step in when individual students are quiet, prompting them to share their thinking. I also step in to lift the conversation as needed.

While I am observer and coach, I take notes. I notice whether students come prepared and whether they are eager to share or are apt to stay quiet. I watch their body language to determine if they are actively listening. I note what type of thinking students share, and how they support that thinking with evidence. I am excited to write notes when I hear students extending their thinking through the help of their peers. This is the purpose of the book club: to broaden students' thinking by introducing alternate ideas.

The notes I take during book club may be formally taken on an observation sheet, or casually written on my conference notecards. I have learned that keeping all my notes in one place makes my life simpler. Therefore, I tend to prefer using my conference notecards. I keep these in a recipe box that has a divider for each student, labeled with his or her name.

Conference notes are written on notecards and organized by student name in a recipe box.

Conferencing

Meeting with partnerships through conferencing allows me to take more of a direct role as teacher and coach. While I try to get around to all partnerships between book club meetings, I select which partners I will meet with based on need. Students who need more support may find me conferencing with them several times between meeting dates. Often times, partnerships will request a conference when they need additional support with the text. The conferencing structure is open to the dynamic flow of modeling and guided practice outlined in the gradual release model. To those of you who would like to learn more about the structure of this type of reading conference, I suggest the book *Guiding Readers and Writers* (Fountas & Pinnell, 2001).

Selecting Texts for Book Clubs

Book clubs tend to fall apart when I try to juggle a multitude of titles. In one classroom of students, I typically have four or five book clubs running at one time. I have finally admitted that this is too much for me to manage if every group is reading a different book. I have also learned that book clubs are more likely to backfire when I allow students in the clubs to select their own books. Therefore, I recommend limiting the number of different books being read at any given time by having more than one group read the same book concurrently, whenever possible. At one time, I actually had all my book clubs reading the same book, and that was probably my most successful book club cycle.

Select your book club books based on what you are working on in read-aloud. This method of book selection allows you to use the read-aloud to build background knowledge about a genre, topic, or author. When readers have ample background knowledge, we are able to stretch them to their highest instructional levels. In addition, staggering the starting dates of read-aloud and book club units ensures that students will not be expected to complete the difficult work of the first quadrant in two books at the same time, which, I've learned the hard way, is too much for young readers to handle. Instead, students will be in the second or third quadrant of the read-aloud book by the time the book club cycle begins, giving them a much more manageable workload.

Notice how, in order to create a stagger, I plan for blocks of time when students will not be meeting in small groups. These blocks of time are shaded gray on the calendar shown below. I know that at the beginning of the year and midyear it is important to explicitly teach and practice key management and procedural mini-lessons. I also know that I will need time during these months to assess students both formally and informally. Blocking off time for this ensures that I have ample time for this important work.

Long Term Planning for the Reading Workshop: First and Second Layer

	Sept.	Oct.	Nov.	Dec.	Jan.	Feb.	March	April	May	June
Read Aloud	Realistic Fiction		Realistic Fiction		Historical Fiction		Nonfiction		Science Fiction	
Book Clubs	Classroom Management and Assessment	Realistic Fiction			Classroom Management and Assessment	Historical Fiction		Nonfiction		

Book club genres are added to the calendar after read-aloud genres are determined.

Independent Practice: The Third Layer of Planning

When the second layer of literacy work is added to the classroom schedule, students are asked to keep track of two chapter books at once, one in read-aloud and one in their book clubs. Adding a third layer, by expecting students to read and complete C. I. A. assignments for an independent book as well, is often asking too much of students. Even adults have trouble keeping track of a multitude of books at once.

Book club work requires students to spend time reading and responding to texts daily. This provides ample time for students to practice strategies and improve fluency and comprehension. I encourage students to keep short text available for independent reading after other work is finished. Examples of short text include nonfiction, magazines, and compilations of short stories and poetry. When setting up my classroom library, I make sure students have a variety of these types of short text to choose from.

While the assignments completed in book clubs give me strong documentation of students' mastery of standards, I also like to see if the C. I. A. work transfers into their independent book choices. Therefore, I schedule one or two opportunities for students to practice C. I. A. strategies in self-selected independent reading. During these times, students are not assigned a book club book. Instead, they are released to do the work independently.

Again, this can be a management nightmare if students select texts of varying lengths and genres, which is why I choose to place parameters on student choices. First, I decide approximately how many pages my students will be able to read in the number of days allotted to this independent project, based on their current stamina. I try to keep all students in texts that are within ten to fifteen pages of the same length. Next, I encourage students to each select a partner, and I help them find double copies of their book choices. Although they will be reading their books independently, they will benefit from the opportunity to touch base with partners throughout the experience.

Once books and partners are chosen, students use a calendar to plan for assignments. All students must finish reading and completing the assignments for quadrant one on the same day, and the same is true for the other quadrants.

Throughout this independent reading project, I am able to pull the entire group to the meeting area for mini-lessons that support their work. Because they are all working in the same section of the text, it doesn't matter that they are reading different books. I plan these mini-lessons based on the C. I. A. framework and on needs assessed during partnership conferences.

Independent reading projects are the last layer in my year-long scope and sequence. After adding this final layer I have mapped out the entire gradual release model over the course of a school year.

Long Term Planning for the Reading Workshop: First, Second, and Third Layer

	Sept.	Oct.	Nov.	Dec.	Jan.	Feb.	March	April	May	June
Read Aloud	Realistic Fiction		Realistic Fiction		Historical Fiction		Nonfiction		Science Fiction	
Book Clubs	*Classroom Management and Assessment*	Realistic Fiction			*Classroom Management and Assessment*	Historical Fiction		Nonfiction		
Independent Project				Realistic Fiction						Free Choice

The final layer is added as teachers plan for independent book projects.

Embracing Shades of Gray

In attempting to give you examples of how the work of the C. I. A. model can be taught and practiced over a school year, I hope I have not implied that teaching is black and white. What works for

one student in a classroom may not work for all. A strategy successfully applied one year may need altering the following year. Rather
than following a clearly set list of rules, our teaching must linger in
shades of gray. Only when we allow for reflection on, evaluation of,
and redesign of our instruction do we arrive at dynamic, passionate,
and spontaneous teaching. I encourage you to remain confident that
your knowledge of significant research combined with your natural
instincts as a teacher will guide you in making the right decisions for
both you and your students.

Conclusion

As I conclude this manuscript, it is summer, and I have vowed that by its end I will read one fun, adult-level book and take time away from reading children's novels and professional texts. Therefore, I have just begun the book *The Help* (Stockett, 2009), a 544-page book. As I begin, I find myself marking the quadrants. The model I have devised for students, the C. I. A. approach, is one that I have transferred over into my personal reading life, and I will never read any other way.

In fact, many of the e-mails I receive from teachers after they have attended the C. I. A. institute describe the impact this approach has made on their own reading lives. One teacher wrote,

> Dear Sarah,
>
> I wanted to tell you that I've been watching your ¾ mark in the books I read (adult books) and it's worked amazingly well. There were a couple of cases where my mouth dropped open as the book's turning point appeared on the page I calculated to be exactly ¾ way through the book. In one case (a murder mystery) the killer proved he really was the killer and opened the lock on the box holding the body on the page that was exactly ¾ way through the book. It's been fun. I have been taking notes on some of the books I read using your guidelines on the first quarter of the book and it's helped me finish two books that I don't think I would have made it through otherwise. They were very complicated and I tired of trying to keep track of it all so I went back in both cases, started over, and took the notes. I then sailed through the books. I like to be able to tell students that I've used this system for myself and that it has helped me be more successful. I think that has more meaning than just telling students to do it.

Her letter proves that this method is transferable into real-world reading contexts; I am truly tickled to have discovered an approach to reading that will carry my students into lifelong reading.

It is true, I often regret not having learned to read this way when I was in school. While I loved reading and always received quality grades in language arts, I know my love of reading would have increased if I had been taught to implement the processes outlined in the C. I. A. model. I certainly would have been better prepared for the challenges of college reading.

Listening to parents whose students have learned the C. I. A. model assures me that this work is making a difference for kids. One parent came to me at the end of the school year, requesting to know the author of the Ember series. She said she planned on giving Ember books to her daughter as a fifth-grade graduation present, knowing that her daughter would love them after her enthusiasm over the first book in the series, *The City of Ember* (DuPrau, 2003). "She came home every night and told us what had happened in the book that day over dinner," described this parent.

After attending the C. I. A. institute in Yakima, Washington, earlier this year, one teacher and parent sent me an e-mail saying,

> I went home after your training and my 6th-grader listened to me rave about the class. He said, "Do you mean CIA mom?" Apparently his teacher taught CIA this year and he loooved it! He said it helped him on the MSP test and MAPS test. He then proceeded to show me his reader's notebook from the year. It sounds like grade 6 is already using your program and as a parent I'm super happy!

Receiving this e-mail was definitely one of my biggest highlights. I find sixth-grade boys to be the most difficult population of students to motivate when it comes to reading. The fact that this e-mail came from the mother of a sixth-grade boy was truly inspiring to me. It proves that a great impact can be made on student achievement when we take time to make the process of reading explicit and motivating for our students.

I know that students are more thoughtful readers as a result of the C. I. A. approach, and those that implement it demonstrate this confidence in their reading skills. I know because as this last school year concluded, students shared these sentiments with me in their letters and cards.

One of my students wrote in a card, "You've helped me so much this year! For the first time I am glad I used a reader's notebook. I've never known so much knowledge in nine months ever before. Thank you for everything! You are the best literacy/5th-grade teacher ever!"

Another student wrote in a letter, "You're a good teacher that has the best strategies when it comes to reading. The strategy that you taught me that has helped me the most is splitting the text into fourths."

Clearly, students see this method as a valuable tool in their learning. For many, their knowledge of these strategies will be the difference between failure and success on the state test, and between failure and success beyond the classroom.

Appendix

Instructional Read-Aloud Framework

Strategy:	Book:
Learning Target/Standard:	
Connection:	Yesterday we were working on…
Teaching:	Today I'm going to teach you…
Modeling:	Watch me as I model how I…
	While I'm reading, I want you to pay attention to how I…
Model #1	
Guided Practice:	Turn and Talk #1
	Turn and Talk #2
Link:	Today and every day I want you to…

Turn and Talk Routine

Partner #1 *Share*	Shares thinking using a turn and talk stem: When the book said _____ I was thinking _____ because _____.
Partner #2 *Respond*	Responds to the partner's thinking using one of the following turn and talk stems: I agree/disagree with you because _____. I am also thinking _____. It sounds like you're saying _____.

Turn and Talk Stems

STRATEGIES	
Connect	When the book said _____ I made a connection. I thought about _____. This helps me understand _____.
Visualize	When the book said _____ I visualized _____. This helps me understand _____.
Predict	When the book said _____ I made a prediction. I think _____ because _____.
Infer	When the book said _____ I inferred _____ because _____. This makes me think _____.
Determine Importance	When the book said _____ I thought this was important because _____. This makes me think _____.

Turn and Talk Stems

SKILLS	
Cause	When the book said _____ I was thinking it might have been caused by _____ because_____.
Effect	When the book said _____ I was thinking this might affect _____ by_____.
Compare	One important way _____ and _____ are alike is_____. This makes me think _____.
Contrast	One important difference between _____and _____ is_____. This makes me think_____.
Main Idea	When the book said _____ I was thinking the main idea of this section is _____ because_____.
Opinion	When the book said _____ I was thinking this shows the author's opinion. I think the author's opinion is _____ because _____.
Problem / Prediction	When the book said _____ I thought the main problem in the story was_____. I predict the problem might be solved by _____ because _____.
Solution / Opinion	In this story, the main problem is_____. The character's plan for solving the problem is_____. I think this is a good/bad solution to the problem because _____.
Drawing Conclusions	After reading _____ and _____ I am concluding _____ because _____.

Turn and Talk Stems

LITERARY ANALYSIS	
Author's Craft	When I read _____ I noticed the author_____. I think the author wants me to _____.
Empathy / Sympathy	When the book said _____ I felt empathy/ sympathy for _____. I felt _____ because _____. This is helping me understand _____.
Mood	When the book said _____ I thought the mood was _____ because _____. This makes me think _____.
Theme	When the book said _____ I was think-ing the theme of the book might be _____ because _____.
Generalizations	When the book said _____ I think the author was trying to tell me that _____ in general _____. This helps me think _____.
Foreshadowing	When I read _____ I thought the author was using foreshadowing. I think the author wants me to predict _____ because _____.
Turning Point	When the book said _____ I thought this was the turning point because _____. This makes me think _____.
Author's Message	When the book said _____ I thought the author's message was _____ because _____.
Evaluating the Author's Message	When the book said _____ I thought the author's message was _____ because _____. I agree/disagree because _____.

Turn and Talk Anecdotal Record Form

NAME	TURN AND TALK NOTES

Layers of Comprehension Work

STRATEGIES	SKILLS	LITERARY ANALYSIS
Ask Questions	• Monitor and clarify • Identify the author's purpose	• Evaluate the author's purpose. Was the author effective?
Form Mental Images	• Describe the physical traits of a character • Describe the setting of a story • Notice literary devices	• Evaluate the author's craft • Distinguish between sympathy and empathy • Notice how the author creates mood
Determine Importance	• Identify the main idea and details • Identify the story sequence • Notice text features • Retell the important events • Identify the speaker/narrator • Explain why the setting is important to the story • Notice text organization • Find evidence of the author's purpose • Distinguish between fact and opinion	• Evaluate the author's craft. Did the author use organization effectively? • Draw conclusions • Make text-to-world connections • Analyze how one plot informs another (within a single text) • Determine the theme and support with text evidence

Make Text-to-Self Connections	• Activate background knowledge	• Make generalizations • Identify how an author makes a story/character believable • Recognize conflict: person vs. person, person vs. nature, person vs. self
Predict	• Cite evidence to support a prediction • Identify the story sequence • Identify a problem/solution • Identify cause and effect	• Recognize foreshadowing • Identify the turning point • Evaluate the solution
Infer	• Cite evidence to support an inference	• Make generalizations • Interpret implied meaning, e.g., metaphor, symbolism • Analyze how characters change over time
Synthesize	• Summarize • Compare and contrast • Formulate a personal response • Draw conclusions • Evaluate the author's effectiveness • Generalize	• Evaluate the author's effectiveness • Formally write in response to reading • Persuade • Make connections across texts • Apply to your life

Vocabulary Mini-Lesson Routine

1.	Introduce the word and high-light morphemes.	*Today our target word is…* If applicable: *What is the root?* *What is the prefix? What does the prefix mean?* *What is the suffix? What does the suffix mean?*
2.	Read the context(s) of the word. Highlight any clues that will help the reader infer the meaning.	*Our target word comes right from our text on page ____. Let's read it together. Are there any clues in the sentence that help us infer what this word means?*
3.	Turn and talk: What does the word _____ mean?	*Based on the clues, what words or phrases describe this word? Turn and talk.*
4.	Share-out and add to chart.	*What did you come up with?* *add accurate examples to the chart
5.	Brainstorm other contexts for this word.	*In what other contexts might we find this word?* *add accurate examples to the chart
6.	Turn and talk: What are opposites of this word?	*What words or phrases describe the opposite of this word? Turn and talk.*
7.	Share-out and add to chart.	*What did you come up with?* *add accurate examples to the chart
8.	I will remember this word…	*How will you remember this word? Draw a picture, or write a phrase that will help you remember this word. Use an example from your own life if possible.*
9.	Link…	*Today and every day I want you to be looking for forms of this word in your reading. I also want you to practice using this word in your talk and in your writing.*

Vocabulary: Making Connections

Target Word:

deserted

Context:

"From the beginning, Jonathan is spooked by the deserted island where his family is camping..." (blurb)

What it is...   **What it is not...**

_____   _____
_____   _____
_____   _____
_____   _____

I'd probably find this word in these contexts (places, events, people, situations):

Text to World

+---+
| |
| |
| |
| |
+---+

I'll remember this word by connecting it to:

(word, phrase, sketch)

+---+
| |
| |
| |
| |
+---+

Vocabulary: Contrasts

Context:

"Moose, panting with fear, huddled beside Jonathan, pawing at Jonathan's shoulder." (p. 23)

"The air was completely still. After the roar of the earthquake, the silence seemed both comforting and ominous." (p. 23)

Target Words:

fear vs. comfort

What it is...

_____

_____

_____

_____

What it is...

_____

_____

_____

_____

I'll remember this word by:

I'll remember this word by:

Genre Chart: Realistic Fiction

REALISTIC FICTION	
Setting	Realistic/believable place Present time
Characters	Made-up characters that are very real and believable The main character changes over time.
Plot	The character must deal with a real-life problem. The character changes over time.
Most important element	Character
Readers will think about:	How the main character changes over time. How the main character overcomes challenges. The main character's beliefs about right and wrong. How the main character's circumstances impact his/her choices.

Genre Chart: Fantasy

FANTASY	
Setting	Fantastical setting • Real world, fantastical elements • Fantastical world, real-world elements Time is relatively unimportant or nonexistent.
Characters	Real or fantastical Good vs. bad, hero vs. villain The main character changes over time (unexpected hero revealed).
Plot	Tension between good and bad, right and wrong
Most important element	Character
Readers will think about:	How the main character changes over time (unexpected hero). How the main character overcomes challenges. How the main character proves goodness. Right vs. wrong, good vs. evil.

Genre Chart: Narrative Nonfiction

NARRATIVE NONFICTION	
Setting	Real place Real time (present or past)
Characters	Key players (important people the author thinks we should know about) Groups of people
Plot	The characters deal with a real-life problem (current or historical event). The characters are changed by the setting and events.
Most important element	Setting
Readers will think about:	Cause and effect. How circumstances shape one's life. The impact of events on our world. Right vs. wrong.

Notebook Entry #1: Finding Story Elements in the Blurb

Blurb:

Characters:

Setting (place):

Setting (time):

Problem:

Predictions:

Retell Summary Frame (Quadrant 1)

Introduction Sentence	*The first one-fourth of the book* _____, *by* _____, *tells/explains* _____ _____.
Body	Describe the most important events from this section of the text. Use transition words such as: *First, next, then, finally,* *First, next, after that, in the end,* *In the beginning, then, after that, finally,*
Conclusion	Describe your thinking about the book. This could be a prediction about what will happen next, an inference about the theme, or a judgment. Use concluding words such as: *In conclusion,* *All in all,* *As you can see,* *It is true,* *I am thinking,*

Adapted from Step Up to Writing *(Auman, 2010)*

Cause and Effect Frame

Introduction Sentence	_____ *caused* __ _____ _____. This sentence should tell the major event and also broadly tell the effect of this event.
Body	Describe several events that happened as a result of the one major event. Include **some** detail. Use transition words such as: *First, next, then, finally,* *First, next, after that, in the end,* *In the beginning, then, after that, finally,*
Conclusion	Describe your thinking about the book. This could be a prediction about what will happen next, an inference about the theme, or a judgment. Use concluding words such as: *In conclusion,* *All in all,* *As you can see,* *It is true,* *I am thinking,* *I predict,*

Adapted from Step Up to Writing *(Auman, 2010)*

Compare/Contrast Frame

Introduction Sentence	If the two things are **more alike** than different, begin by saying: _____ is _____ and _____ is _____, but for the most part they are similar._ If the two things are **more different** than alike, begin by saying: _____ and _____ both _____, but overall they are very different._
Body	Explain the ways these two things are either alike or different. Use transition words such as: _First, second, third,_ _One way, another way, also,_ _First, also, in addition,_
Conclusion	Restate your thinking. Start with one of the following phrases: _In conclusion,_ _All in all,_ _As you can see,_ _It is true,_ _To sum up,_

Adapted from Step Up to Writing _(Auman, 2010)_

Problem/Solution/Opinion Frame

Introduction Sentences	State the problem and solution. Tell whether you agree or disagree with how the problem was solved.
Body	Give strong evidence that supports your opinion. (Evidence can come from the text and/or your own life.)
Conclusion	Restate your thinking. Start with one of the following phrases: *In conclusion,* *All in all,* *As you can see,* *It is true,* *To sum up,*

Adapted from Step Up to Writing *(Auman, 2010)*

Collect Evidence

Line of thinking: _____

_____

_____

Evidence Collection Box

Turning Point Writing

I think the turning point of the book is…

This will change the plot because…

I think this event tells me that the author's message is…

I predict…

Formal Reflection Frame

PARAGRAPH 1: SYNTHESIS SUMMARY	
Introduction Sentence	*The book _____, by _____, tells about _____.*
Body	Tell the events of the book in 5–7 sentences.
Concluding Sentence	*In conclusion, _____ _____.*
PARAGRAPH 2: AUTHOR'S MESSAGE	
Introduction Sentence	*I think the author's message is _____.*
Body	State the evidence from the book that supports this thinking.
Concluding Sentence	*It is clear, _____ _____.*
PARAGRAPH 3: EVALUATE THE AUTHOR'S MESSAGE	
Introduction Sentence	*I agree/disagree with the author's message.* *I think _____ _____.*
Body	State evidence from outside sources or your own life that supports your thinking.
Concluding Sentence	*As you can see, _____ _____.*

C. I. A. S. Student Checklist

C	**Collect Thinking: Quadrant 1** What genre is your book? Realistic Fiction Historical Fiction Fantasy Non-Fiction Other: _____ **Get the story in your head by identifying the key story elements:** **Character** ____ List the main characters of the book and information you learn about them. **Setting** ____ Make a setting map or setting clues list. **Plot** ____ List the main events for each chapter in your reader's notebook. Hint: There will be 1-2 main events/chapter. ____ Write a retell summary of the first ¼ of your book. __| **Interpret the Book: Quadrant 2** ____ Narrow your focus to what is important to this genre: _____ ____ Look for key repeated words: _____ ____ Consider possible themes and select one that you can support with text evidence. ____ Make an evidence collection box. **Interpret the Book: Quadrant 3** ____ Add evidence to the evidence collection box. ____ Identify foreshadowing and stop to make a prediction: ____ When the book said____ I made I prediction. I think____ because ____. ____ Stop and identify the turning point. ____ Reflect on the turning point: Turning Point Writing

A	**Apply to Your Life: Quadrant 4**
	After reading, write a reflection in your reader's notebook:
	    Paragraph 1: Summarize the book in about 6 - 8 sentences.
	        Paragraph 2: What is the author's message?
	            What evidence from the book supports this thinking?
	        Paragraph 3: Do you agree with the message? Why?
	            Extra: How has your life or your thoughts about the world been impacted by this book?

S	**Share After Reading** • Write a book review • Find someone else who has read the book and compare thoughts about the book • Write a letter to the author of the book sharing your thinking and why you liked it • Write a literary essay • Other idea:

References

Chapter Books, Picture Books, and Video Reference List

Avi (1995). *Poppy.* New York, NY: Avon Books, Inc.

Creech, S. (1994). *Walk two moons.* New York, NY: Scholastic Paperbacks.

DiCamillo, K. (2000). *Because of Winn Dixie.* Somerville, MA: Candlewick Press.

D'Lacey, C. (2007). *Firestar.* New York, NY: Scholastic Paperbacks.

DuPrau, J. (2003). *The city of Ember.* New York, NY: Yearling.

Henkes, K. (2005). *Olive's ocean.* New York, NY: Greenwillow Books.

Hesse, K. (1999). *Out of the dust.* New York, NY: Scholastic Paperbacks.

Hunter, E. (2003). *Into the wild.* New York, NY: Harper Collins.

Hurwitz, J. (2002). *One small dog.* New York, NY: Harper Collins.

Kehret, P. (1996). *Earthquake terror.* New York, NY: Puffin Books.

Kenan, G. (Director). (2009). *City of Ember* [DVD]. United States: Twentieth Century Fox.

MacLachlan, P. (1993). *Baby.* New York, NY: Yearling.

Morpurgo, M. (2003). *Kensuke's kingdom.* New York, NY: Scholastic Paperbacks.

Naylor, P.R. (1991). *Shiloh.* New York, NY: Atheneum.

Osborne, W. & Osborne, M.P. (2000). *Knights and castles: Magic tree house research guide.* New York, NY: Random House, Inc.

Rowling, J. K. (1997). *Harry Potter and the sorcerer's stone.* New York, NY: Scholastic Paperbacks.

Sachar, L. (1998). *Holes.* New York, NY: Dell Yearling.

Spinelli, J. (1990). *Maniac Magee.* New York, NY: Scholastic Paperbacks.

Stanley, J. (1992). *Children of the Dust Bowl: The true story of the school at Weedpatch Camp.* New York, NY: Crown Publishers.

Stockett, K. (2009). *The help.* New York, NY: Penguin Books.

Winthrop, E. (1985). *The castle in the attic.* New York, NY: Bantam Doubleday Dell Books for Young Readers.

Winthrop, E. (1994). *The battle for the castle.* New York, NY: Yearling.

Young, E. (1992). *Seven blind mice.* New York, NY: Penguin Books.

Professional References

ACT, Inc. (2006). *Reading between the lines: What the ACT reveals about college readiness in reading,* Kindle edition. Iowa City, IA: Author.

ACT, Inc. (2009). *The condition of college readiness 2009.* Iowa City, IA: Author.

Adams, M. J. (2009). The challenge of advanced texts: The interdependence of reading and learning. In E. H. Hiebert (Ed.), *Reading more, reading better: Are American students reading enough of the right stuff?* (pp. 163–189). New York, NY: Guilford.

Angelillo, J. (2003). *Writing about reading: From book talk to literary essays, grades 3–8.* Portsmouth, NH: Heinemann.

Arthur, K. (1994). *How to study your Bible: The lasting rewards of the inductive method.* Eugene, OR: Harvest House Publishers.

Auman, M. (2010). *Step up to writing.* Longmount, Colorado: Sopriswest.

Beaver, J. & Carter, M. (2005). *Developmental Reading Assessment.* Lebanon, IN: Pearson.

Beck, I. L., McKeown, M. G., & Kucan, L. (2002). *Bringing words to life: Robust vocabulary instruction.* New York, NY: The Guilford Press.

Bernard, B. C. (1988). *James Bryce and St. Louis: A bibliographic introduction to the writings of James Bryce, May 10, 1988.* Granite City, IL: B.C. Bernard.

Bloom, B. S. (1956). *Taxonomy of educational objectives, handbook I: The cognitive domain.* New York: David McKay Co. Inc.

Buckner, A. E. (2009). *Notebook connections: Strategies for the reader's notebook.* Portland, ME: Stenhouse Publishers.

Calkins, L. M. (2001). *The art of teaching reading.* New York, NY: Longman.

Common Core State Standards Initiative. (2010). *Common Core State Standards for English language arts & literacy in history/social studies, science and technical subjects, appendix A.* Washington, DC: Author.

Cunningham, P. M., & Allington, R. L. (2007). *Classrooms that work: They can all read and write.* New York, NY: Pearson.

Fletcher, R. & Portalupi, J. (2001). *Writing workshop: The essential guide.* Portsmouth, NH: Heinemann.

Fountas, I. C. & Pinnell, G. S. (1996). *Guided reading: Good first teaching for all children.* Portsmouth, NH: Heinemann.

Fountas, I. C. & Pinnell, G. S. (2001). *Guiding readers and writers grades 3–6: Teaching comprehension, genre, and content literacy.* Portsmouth, NH: Heinemann.

Fountas, I. C., & Pinnell, G. S. (2006). *Teaching for comprehension and fluency: Thinking, talking and writing about reading, K–8.* Portsmouth, NH: Heinemann.

Harvey, S., & Goudvis, A. (2000). *Strategies that work: Teaching comprehension to enhance understanding.* Portland, ME: Stenhouse Publishers.

Lewis, J. & Moorman, G. (2007). *Adolescent literacy instruction: Policies and promising practices.* Newark, DE: International Reading Association.

McLaughlin, M. & DeVoogd, G. (2004). Critical literacy as comprehension: Expanding reader response. *Journal of Adolescent & Adult Literacy, 48.1,* 52–62.

National Institute of Child Health and Human Development. (2000). *Report of the National Reading Panel. Teaching children to read: An evidence-based assessment of the scientific research literature on reading and its implications for reading instruction* (NIH Publication No. 00-4769). Washington, DC: U.S. Government Printing Office.

Pearson, P. D., & Gallagher, M. C. (1983). The instruction of reading comprehension. *Contemporary Educational Psychology, 8,* 317–344.

RAND Reading Study Group. (2002). *Reading for understanding: Toward an R & D program in reading comprehension.* Santa Monica, CA: RAND.

Rasinski, T. V. (2003). *The fluent reader.* New York, NY: Scholastic Professional Books.

Schmoker, M. (2011). *Focus: Elevating the essentials to radically improve student learning.* Alexandria, VA: Association for Supervision & Curriculum Development.

Shanahan, T. (2011, May). 10 things every teacher should know about reading comprehension. Speech presented at the Plain Talk About Reading Conference, Orlando, FL.

Stiggins, R. J., Arter, J. A., Chappuis, J. & Chappuis, S. (2006). *Classroom assessment for student learning: Doing it right – using it well.* Princeton, NJ: Educational Testing Service.

Taberski, S. (2000). *On solid ground: Strategies for teaching reading K–3.* Portsmouth, NH: Heinemann.

Thomas, A. (2011, May). Increasing comprehension with higher order thinking. Speech presented at the Plain Talk About Reading Conference, Orlando, FL.

Tovani, C. (2000). *I read it, but I don't get it: Comprehension strategies for adolescent readers.* Portland, ME: Stenhouse Publishers.

Wood Ray, K. (2002). *What you know by heart: How to develop curriculum for your writing workshop.* Portsmouth, NH: Heinemann.

Wood Ray, K. (2006). *Study driven: A framework for planning units of study in the writing workshop.* Portsmouth, NH: Heinemann.

Zemelman, S., Daniels, H., & Hyde, A. (2005). *Best practice: Today's standards for teaching & learning in America's schools.* Portsmouth, NH: Heinemann.

Read Side by Side

Literacy Publications & Consulting

Contact Sarah Collinge

Sarah Collinge offers workshops, seminars, consulting and coaching to schools throughout the United States. Visit her Web site at **www.readsidebyside.com** to invite her to your building, district or region.

You may also email Sarah at **info@readsidebyside.com**.

Additional Publications

Sarah has also designed units of study that utilize the C. I. A. approach. These units provide curriculum for listening comprehension, vocabulary, speaking, and writing. Aligned to the Common Core State Standards, these units have been proven to raise state test scores in classrooms throughout Washington State. Units can be purchased on Sarah's website: **www.readsidebyside.com**.